PREFAB ARCHITECTURE

ARCHITECTURE PRÉFABRIQUÉE

PREFAB ARCHITECTURE

PREFAB ARCHITECTUUR

VIVIENDAS PREFABRICADAS

PREFAB ARCHITECTURE

VIVENDAS PRÉ-FABRICADAS

PREFABRICERAD ARKITEKTUR

KÖNEMANN

© 2018 koenemann.com GmbH
www.koenemann.com

ÉDITIONS
PLACE DES
VICTOIRES

© Éditions Place des Victoires
6, rue du Mail – 75002 Paris
www.victoires.com
ISBN : 978-2-8099-1501-3
Dépôt légal : 2ᵉ trimestre 2018

Editorial project:
LOFT Publications
Barcelona, Spain
loft@loftpublications.com
www.loftpublications.com

Editorial coordinator:
Aitana Lleonart Triquell

Assistant to editorial coordination:
Ana Marques

Editor and text:
Marta Serrats

Art director:
Mireia Casanovas Soley

Design and layout coordination:
Claudia Martínez Alonso

Layout:
Cristina Simó Perales

Translations:
Cillero & de Motta

ISBN: 978-3-7419-2054-7

Printed in China by Shenzhen Hua Xin Colour-printing & Platemaking Co., Ltd.

Ecology and sustainability are concepts that currently enjoy great influence, and have a bearing on many spheres of life today, especially that of architecture. We all agree with the theories on global warming and with the need to reduce our CO_2 emissions and ensure that our lifestyles are more respectful of the environment. As far as architecture is concerned, there are some significant changes and developments, but as yet they are still insufficient. Without going any further, in the sphere of residential architecture the number of houses is already on the rise thanks to the growing population and, as a result, there is also increased consumption of raw materials and greater environmental costs for transportation. It is therefore imperative to search for new building solutions that are environmentally friendly and lead to a reduction in the consumption of materials and energy, including both active and passive systems. One of these construction solutions are prefabricated housing.

Mass production of housing has a long tradition in Europe, especially in the more industrialized northern countries, and in the United States, with the so-called "McMansions" and the expansion of prefabricated modules in states with greatest seismic risk, such as California.

Sometimes this type of architecture arose from political and economic reasons, which prompted the construction of prefabricated homes in the Eastern bloc countries during the 1960s and 1970s. In other cases, Germany, Austria and Scandinavia -the very ecological mindset and demanding standards converted these countries into the champions of the eco-architecture revolution we are experiencing today.

The prejudices that surround prefabricated systems, such as a symbol of cheap, unattractive and even less exclusive construction method (with catalog houses, as an exponent), are changing. By using new technologies and advanced CAD/CAM/CAE systems, the current models of modern style are appreciated by an ever wider audience. The supply has increased and, better yet, it has diversified.

The ecological, social and economic consequences of these systems are obvious: you get a reduction in execution time, a more uniform and perfect finish, and a reduced environmental impact and occupational hazard at the site. As a bonus, the three most common prefabrication systems (wood, steel and concrete) involve a lower cost for the manufacturer and the final buyer.

The global expansion of prefabricated systems explains that major distributors of household sector such as IKEA (www.boklok.com) and MUJI (www.muji.net/ie) already offer their own models. We can also find other local initiatives in The Netherlands (www.spacebox.nl), the United Kingdom (www.containercity.com) and Spain (www.habidite.com).

The following pages showcase residential solutions based on an optimal and attractive design, with a production attracted by the latest technologies and strong environmental ambition.

L'écologie et la durabilité sont des concepts très présents dans l'actualité, qui englobent de nombreux domaines de notre vie et plus particulièrement celui de l'architecture. Tout le monde est d'accord sur les théories du réchauffement de la planète et sur la nécessité de réduire les émissions de CO_2, en ayant pour cela des styles de vie plus respectueux de l'environnement. Dans le domaine de l'architecture, des modifications et des progrès importants sont en cours mais ils restent encore insuffisants. Rien que dans le domaine de l'architecture résidentielle, on observe déjà une augmentation du parc de logements découlant de l'accroissement de la population, ce qui entraîne une plus grande consommation de matières premières et une augmentation des coûts environnementaux liés aux transports. Il est donc nécessaire d'envisager de nouvelles solutions écologiques pour la construction qui réduisent la consommation de matériaux et d'énergie, aussi bien des systèmes actifs que passifs. Les habitations préfabriquées constituent l'une de ces solutions constructives.

La production en série d'habitations a une longue tradition aussi bien en Europe, notamment dans les pays du nord plus industrialisés, qu'aux États-Unis, avec ses célèbres *McMansions* et l'expansion de modules préfabriqués dans les états qui présentent un plus grand risque sismique comme la Californie.

Ce type d'architecture est parfois apparu pour des raisons politiques et économiques, comme dans les pays du bloc de l'Est, où la construction de résidences préfabriquées s'est accrue dans les années soixante et soixante-dix. Dans d'autres cas, comme en Allemagne, en Autriche et en Scandinavie, la propre mentalité écologique et une réglementation plus exigeante ont placé ces pays à la tête de la révolution *éco-architecturale* que nous vivons actuellement.

Les préjugés qui entourent les systèmes préfabriqués, considérés comme un symbole de construction bon marché, avec peu de charme et encore moins d'exclusivité (les habitations sont vendues sur catalogue), sont en train de changer. Grâce à l'utilisation de nouvelles technologies et aux applications informatiques avancées CAD/CAM/CAE, les modèles présentés actuellement de style moderne sont appréciés par un public de plus en plus large. L'offre a augmenté et s'est même diversifiée.

Ces systèmes offrent de nombreux avantages écologiques, sociaux et économiques : ils permettent de réduire la durée de construction, offrent des finitions plus uniformes et parfaites et ont un impact moindre pour l'environnement et les risques encourus sur le lieu de travail. Les trois systèmes de préfabrication les plus répandus (bois, acier et béton) permettent également de réduire les coûts pour le fabricant et l'acheteur final.

L'essor des systèmes préfabriqués au niveau mondial explique pourquoi de grands distributeurs spécialisés dans les articles de la maison comme IKEA (www.boklok.com) et MUJI (www.muji.net/ie) proposent déjà leurs propres modèles. D'autres initiatives ont également été mises en place au niveau local, comme en Hollande (www.spacebox.nl), en Angleterre (www.containercity.com) ou en Espagne (www.habidite.com).

Les pages suivantes présentent des solutions résidentielles avec un design optimal et séduisant, une construction basée sur les dernières technologies et une nette vocation écologique.

Umweltschutz und Nachhaltigkeit sind heutzutage sehr einflussreiche Konzepte, die viele Bereiche unseres Lebens, wie auch speziell die Architektur, betreffen. Alle stimmen mit den Theorien der globalen Erwärmung und der Notwendigkeit, die CO_2 Abgaben zu senken und umweltbewusstere Lebensstile zu führen, überein. Im Bereich der Architektur erfolgen schon bedeutende Veränderungen und Fortschritte, die aber immer noch unzureichend sind. Bei der Wohnhausarchitektur ist ein Anstieg des Wohnungsparks aufgrund des Bevölkerungsanstiegs zu verzeichnen. Parallel dazu erhöhen sich der Rohmaterialverbrauch und die Umweltkosten des Transports. Aus diesem Grund müssen neue ökologische – egal ob aktive oder passive – Lösungen für den Bau betrachtet werden, um den Material- und Energieverbrauch zu senken. Eine dieser baulichen Lösungen sind Fertighäuser.

Die Serienproduktion dieser Häuser besitzt in Europa und dort vor allem in den industrialisierteren nördlichen Ländern, wie auch in den Vereinigten Staaten mit den sogenannten *McMansions*, eine große Tradition. Dazu kommt die Anzahl an Fertighäusern in Staaten mit höherer Erdbebengefahr wie Kalifornien.

In anderen Fällen entstand diese Architektur aus politischen und wirtschaftlichen Gründen, wie z. B. der Fertighausbau in den Ostblockländern der sechziger und siebziger Jahre. In Deutschland, Österreich und Skandinavien machten deren eigene umweltbewusste Mentalität sowie strengere Vorschriften diese Länder zu Vorreitern der heutigen *ökoarchitektonischen* Revolution.

Die Vorurteile, mit denen die Fertigbausysteme als Symbole einer billigen, kaum attraktiven und insbesondere nicht exklusiven Bauweise (wie die Häuser per Katalog als Exponenten) bezichtigt werden, ändern sich jedoch. Dank des Einsatzes neuer Technologien und der modernen CAD/CAM/CAE Systeme, finden die aktuellen Modelle mit modernem Stil einen immer breiteren Anklang. Das Angebot ist gestiegen, oder besser gesagt, es hat sich diversifiziert.

Die ökologischen, sozialen und wirtschaftlichen Vorteile dieser Systeme liegen auf der Hand: Die Bauzeit wird kürzer, die Ausführungen sind gleichmäßiger und perfekter und die Auswirkungen auf die Umwelt wie auch die Arbeitsgefahr auf der Baustelle reduzieren sich. Als zusätzlicher Vorteil bieten die drei am meisten verbreiteten Fertigbausysteme (Holz, Stahl und Beton) geringere Kosten für Hersteller und Endkunden.

Die globale Ausdehnung der Fertigbausysteme erklärt auch, warum die großen Händler der Heimbranche wie IKEA (www.boklok.com) und MUJI (www.muji.net/ie) schon ihre eigenen Modelle anbieten. Man kann aber auch andere lokalere Initiativen in Holland (www.spacebox.nl), England (www.containercity.com) oder Spanien (www.habidite.com) finden.

Auf den folgenden Seiten sind Wohnlösungen auf der Grundlage eines optimalen und attraktiven Designs mit einer Produktion dargestellt, die sich für die neuesten Technologien und ein klares, umweltbewusstes Bestreben einsetzt.

De concepten ecologie en duurzaamheid zijn tegenwoordig van grote invloed op allerlei terreinen van het leven, met name in de architectuur. Iedereen is het wel eens over de theorieën over de opwarming van de aarde, de noodzaak om de CO_2-uitstoot te verminderen en meer respect voor het milieu aan de dag te leggen in onze leefstijl. Op het gebied van de architectuur zijn belangrijke veranderingen gaande en wordt grote vooruitgang geboekt, maar deze zijn helaas nog niet voldoende. Alleen al binnen de woningarchitectuur zien we een uitbreiding door de groeiende bevolking, met als gevolg een groter grondstoffengebruik en een grotere belasting van het milieu vanwege het transport. Om die reden is het noodzakelijk te zoeken naar nieuwe ecologische oplossingen voor de bouw die het verbruik van grondstoffen en energie terugbrengen, of dat nu met actieve of passieve systemen gebeurt. Een van die oplossingen zijn geprefabriceerde woningen.

Serieproductie van woningen kent een lage traditie in zowel Europa, en dan met name in de meest geïndustrialiseerde noordelijke landen, als de Verenigde Staten met hun zogenaamde *McMansions* en de toename van prefabmodulen in de staten met een vergroot risico op aardbevingen, zoals Californië.

In sommige gevallen kwam dit type architectuur voort uit politieke en economische redenen; zo nam de bouw van prefabwoningen in de Oostbloklanden vlucht in de jaren zestig en zeventig van de vorige eeuw. In andere gevallen, zoals in Duitsland, Oostenrijk en Scandinavië, veranderden de eigen ecologische mentaliteit en strengere normen in de betreffende landen in vaandeldragers van de 'ecoarchitectonische' revolutie waar we momenteel middenin zitten.

De vooroordelen omtrent prefabsystemen – ze zouden voor goedkope, onaantrekkelijke en minder exclusieve bouw staan (met als dieptepunt de postorderwoningen) – zijn op hun retour. Dankzij nieuwe technologieën en de geavanceerde CAD/CAM/CAE-systemen is er een steeds groter publiek dat de huidige, moderne modellen weet te waarderen. Het aanbod is uitgebreid en, beter nog, diverser geworden.

De ecologische, sociale en economische voordelen van deze systemen zijn duidelijk: de bouwtijd is korter, de afwerking is uniformer en strakker, de belasting van het milieu is minder groot en het risico op ongelukken op de bouwplaats is kleiner. Bijkomend voordeel is dat de meest gebruikte prefabconstructies (hout, staal en beton) minder kosten voor zowel de fabrikant als de uiteindelijke koper met zich meebrengen.

De wereldwijde uitbreiding van prefabsystemen verklaart ook waarom de grote ketens en groothandelaars in de woonsector, zoals IKEA (www.boklok.com) en MUJI (www.muji.net/ie) hun eigen modellen inmiddels op de markt brengen. Ook zien we initiatieven op meer lokaal niveau in Nederland (www.spacebox.nl), Engeland (www.containercity.com) en Spanje (www.habidite.com).

De volgende pagina's laten woonoplossingen zien die zijn gebaseerd op een aantrekkelijk ontwerp van topkwaliteit en zijn gebouwd met behulp van de nieuwste technologie en een stevige dosis ecologisch ambitie.

Ecología y sostenibilidad son en la actualidad conceptos de gran influencia y abarcan muchos ámbitos de nuestra vida, especialmente el de la arquitectura. Todo el mundo está de acuerdo con las teorías sobre el calentamiento global y con la necesidad de reducir las emisiones de CO_2 y de llevar estilos de vida más respetuosos con el medio ambiente. En el campo de la arquitectura se están realizando cambios y avances importantes, pero que aún son insuficientes. Sólo en el campo de la arquitectura residencial ya se produce un aumento del parque de viviendas derivado del incremento de la población y, en consecuencia, se produce también un mayor consumo de materias primas y un incremento de los costes ambientales del transporte. Por lo tanto, es necesario considerar nuevas soluciones ecológicas para la construcción que reduzcan el consumo de materiales y de energía, ya sean sistemas activos o pasivos. Una de estas soluciones constructivas son las viviendas prefabricadas.

La producción en serie de viviendas tiene una larga tradición tanto en Europa, sobre todo en los países del Norte más industrializados, como en Estados Unidos, con las llamadas *McMansions* y la expansión de módulos prefabricados en los estados con mayor riesgo sísmico, como California.

En ocasiones, este tipo de arquitectura surgió por razones políticas y económicas, lo que impulsó la construcción de residencias prefabricadas en los países del bloque del Este durante las décadas de los sesenta y los setenta. En otros casos –Alemania, Austria y Escandinavia–, la propia mentalidad ecológica y una normativa más exigente convirtió a esos países en abanderados de la revolución «ecoarquitectónica» que vivimos hoy en día.

Los prejuicios que envuelven a los sistemas prefabricados, como símbolo de construcción barata, poco atractiva y menos aún exclusiva (con las viviendas por catálogo como exponente), están cambiando. Gracias al uso de nuevas tecnologías y a los avanzados sistemas de CAD/CAM/CAE, los modelos actuales de estilo moderno son apreciados por un público cada vez más amplio. La oferta se ha incrementado y, mejor aún, se ha diversificado.

Las ventajas ecológicas, sociales y económicas de estos sistemas son evidentes: se consigue una reducción del tiempo de ejecución, unos acabados más uniformes y perfectos, y un menor impacto ambiental y de riesgo laboral en el emplazamiento. Como ventaja adicional, los tres sistemas de prefabricación más extendidos (madera, acero y hormigón) conllevan un gasto menor para el fabricante y el comprador final.

La expansión global de los sistemas prefabricados explica que grandes distribuidores del sector del hogar como IKEA (www.boklok.com) y MUJI (www.muji.net/ie) ya ofrezcan sus propios modelos. También podemos encontrar otras iniciativas más locales en los Países Bajos (www.spacebox.nl), Reino Unido (www.containercity.com) o España (www.habidite.com).

Las páginas siguientes nos muestran soluciones residenciales basadas en un diseño óptimo y atractivo, con una producción atraída por las últimas tecnologías y una firme ambición ecológica.

Ecologia e sostenibilità sono attualmente concetti di grande peso e interessano molti aspetti della nostra vita, in particolare l'architettura. Tutti sono d'accordo con le teorie sul surriscaldamento globale e con la necessità di ridurre le emissioni di CO_2, abbracciando stili di vita più rispettosi verso l'ambiente. Nel campo dell'architettura sono in corso cambiamenti e significativi progressi, ma risultano ancora insufficienti. Solo nel settore dell'architettura residenziale si verifica già un aumento dell'offerta residenziale, prodotto dalla crescita della popolazione, e di conseguenza aumenta anche il consumo di materie prime e i costi ambientali di trasporto. Pertanto, è necessario esplorare nuove soluzioni a salvaguardia dell'ambiente per la costruzione, riducendo il consumo di materiali ed energia, sia mediante sistemi attivi che passivi. Una di queste soluzioni edilizie sono le abitazioni prefabbricate.

La produzione in serie di abitazioni ha una lunga tradizione in Europa, specialmente nei paesi settentrionali industrializzati, e negli Stati Uniti, con le cosiddette *McMansions* e la diffusione di moduli prefabbricati negli stati con più alto rischio sismico come California.

A volte questo tipo di architettura nasce da ragioni politiche ed economiche, come quelle che hanno indotto la costruzione di case prefabbricate nei paesi del blocco orientale negli anni Sessanta e Settanta. In altri casi, come Germania, Austria e Scandinavia, una mentalità ecologica e una normativa più esigente hanno trasformato questi paesi nei promotori della rivoluzione *eco-architettonica* che si sta diffondendo al giorno d'oggi.

I pregiudizi che circondano i sistemi di costruzione prefabbricati, come simbolo di costruzione a buon mercato, poco attraente e ancor meno esclusiva (le case su catalogo in primis), stanno cambiando. Impiegando tecnologie nuove e gli avanzati sistemi CAD/CAM/CAE, gli attuali modelli di stile moderno sono apprezzati da un pubblico sempre più ampio. L'offerta è aumentata e, meglio ancora, si è diversificata.

I vantaggi ecologici, sociali ed economici di questi sistemi sono evidenti: si ottiene una riduzione dei tempi di esecuzione, finiture più uniformi e perfette, e un impatto ambientale ridotto con meno rischi di natura professionale presso il cantiere. Oltretutto, i tre sistemi di prefabbricazione più comuni (legno, acciaio e cemento) comportano un minor costo di trasporto per il produttore e per il compratore finale.

La diffusione globale dei sistemi prefabbricati spiega il motivo per cui grandi distributori del settore dell'arredamento come IKEA (www.boklok.com) e MUJI (www.muji.net/ie) offrono già i loro modelli. Si possono anche trovare altre iniziative locali nei Paesi Bassi (www.spacebox.nl), in Inghilterra (www.containercity.com) o in Spagna (www.habidite.com).

Le pagine seguenti mostrano soluzioni abitative basate su un design ottimale e attraente, con una produzione all'insegna delle più recenti tecnologie e con un solido compromesso ambientale.

Ecologia e sustentabilidade são actualmente conceitos de grande influência e abarcam muitas áreas da nossa vida, especialmente o da arquitectura. Todos estão de acordo com as teorias sobre o aquecimento global, com a necessidade de reduzir as emissões de CO_2 e de levar estilos de vida que respeitem mais o meio ambiente. No campo da arquitectura estão a realizar- -se alterações e avanços importantes, mas que ainda são insuficientes. Só no campo da arquitectura residencial já se produz um aumento dos conjuntos habitacionais derivado ao aumento da população e, como consequência, produz-se também um maior consumo de matérias-primas e aumentam os custos ambientais do transporte. É portanto necessário criar novas soluções ecológicas para a construção que reduzam o consumo de materiais e de energia, quer sejam sistemas activos ou passivos. Uma destas soluções construtivas são as casas pré-fabricadas.

A produção em série de casas tem uma longa tradição tanto na Europa, sobretudo nos países do Norte mais industrializados, como nos Estados Unidos, com as chamadas *McMansions* e a expansão de módulos pré-fabricados nos estados com maior risco sísmico como a Califórnia.

Em certas ocasiões, este tipo de arquitectura surgiu por razões políticas e económicas, o que impulsionou a construção de residências pré-fabricadas nos países do bloco do Este durante as décadas dos sessenta e setenta. Noutros casos – Alemanha, Áustria e Escandinávia – a própria mentalidade ecológica e uma lei mais exigente converteu esses países em pioneiros da revolução *eco-arquitectónica* que vivemos hoje em dia.

As desvantagens que envolvem os sistemas pré-fabricados, como símbolo de construção barata, pouco atraente e menos ainda exclusiva (com as casas por catálogo, como expoente), estão a mudar. Graças à utilização das novas tecnologias e aos avançados sistemas de CAD/CAM/CAE, os modelos actuais de estilo moderno são apreciados por um público cada vez mais vasto. A oferta aumentou e, melhor ainda, diversificou-se.

As vantagens ecológicas, sociais e económicas destes sistemas são evidentes: consegue-se uma redução do tempo de execução, acabamentos mais uniformes e perfeitos, e um menor impacto ambiental e de risco laboral no local. Como vantagem adicional, os três sistemas de prefabricação mais difundidos (madeira, aço e betão) acarretam um menor gasto para o fabricante e para o comprador final.

A expansão global dos sistemas pré-fabricados explica que grandes distribuidores do sector do lar como IKEA (www.boklok.com) e MUJI (www.muji.net/ie) já ofereçam os seus próprios modelos. Podemos também encontrar outras iniciativas mais locais na Holanda (www.spacebox.nl), Inglaterra (www.containercity.com) ou Espanha (www.habidite.com).

As páginas seguintes mostram-nos soluções residenciais baseadas num desenho óptimo e atraente, com uma produção aliciada pelas últimas tecnologias e uma firme ambição ecológica.

Ekologi och hållbarhet är för närvarande begrepp som har stor påverkan och som omfattar många områden i våra liv, särskilt arkitekturen. Alla är överens om teorierna om den globala uppvärmningen och nödvändigheten att minska utsläppen av koldioxid och att anamma en mer miljövänlig livsstil. Inom arkitekturen sker förändringar och viktiga framsteg, men de är fortfarande otillräckliga. Bara inom bostadsarkitekturen produceras ett ökat antal bostäder till följd av befolkningsökningen och därmed ökar även konsumtionen av råvaror och transporter vilket påverkar miljön. Alltså är det nödvändigt att beakta nya miljövänliga lösningar för byggbranschen, som minskar konsumtionen av material och energi, oavsett om det är aktiva eller passiva system. En av dessa konstruktiva lösningar är monteringsfärdiga bostäder.

Serietillverkning av bostäder har en lång tradition både i Europa, framförallt i länderna i norr som är mer industrialiserade, och i USA, med de så kallade *McMansions* och utbredningen av monteringsfärdiga moduler i stater med större jordbävningsrisk, som Kalifornien.

I vissa fall uppstod denna typ av arkitektur av politiska och ekonomiska skäl, vilket stimulerade byggnation av monteringsfärdiga bostäder i öststaterna under 60- och 70-talen. I andra fall, som Tyskland, Österrike och Skandinavien, har miljömedvetenheten och en mer krävande lagstiftning i dessa länder gjort att de har blivit företrädare för den *eko- arkitektoniska*revolutionen som vi upplever idag.

Fördomarna mot de monteringsfärdiga systemen, som symbol för billig konstruktion med mindre attraktion och ännu mindre exklusivitet (med bostäderna i katalog, som modeller) håller på att förändras. Tack vare användningen av ny teknologi och avancerade CAD/CAM/CAE-system, uppskattas de aktuella modellerna med modern stil av en allt bredare publik. Utbudet har ökat och blivit allt mer varierat.

De ekologiska, sociala och ekonomiska fördelarna med dessa system är uppenbara: Man åstadkommer kortare tider för uppförande, mer enhetlig och perfekt finish, mindre miljöpåverkan och mindre arbetsrisker vid placeringen. Ytterligare en fördel är att de tre vanligast förekommande materialen för monteringsfärdiga bostäder (trä, stål och betong) medför mindre utgifter för tillverkaren och den slutgiltige köparen.

Den globala utbredningen av monteringsfärdiga system förklarar varför de stora distributörerna inom bostadssektorn, som IKEA(www.boklok.com) och MUJI (www.muji.net/ie) redan erbjuder sina egna modeller. Vi kan också hitta andra mer lokala initiativ i Holland (www.spacebox.nl), England (www.containercity.com) och Spanien (www.habidite.com).

Följande sidor visar bostadslösningar som baseras på optimal och attraktiv design, med en produktion som attraheras av den senaste tekniken och en orubblig ekologisk ambition.

HOUSE **M**

Caramel Architekten
Linz, Austria
© Otto Hainzl/Augment

This cube, 108 m² (1,162 sq ft) with a 31 m² (333 sq ft) terrace, has a 12 x 12 m (39 x 39 ft) square floor plan, closed on two of its façades to prevent exposure to neighboring parcels. The shell of the cube is made up of synthetic membranes: EPDM for the roof and PVC with white Teflon for façades. Construction lasted nine months.

Cette construction de 108 m² présente une terrasse de 31 m², une base carrée (12 x 12 m) , ainsi que deux façades qui la cachent des parcelles voisines. L'enveloppe du cube est constituée de membranes synthétiques : EPDM pour la toiture et PVC, avec une finition de téflon blanc, pour les façades. La construction a duré neuf mois.

Dieser 108 m² große Würfel mit einer 31 m² großen Terrasse besitzt einen quadratischen Grundriss (12 x 12 m), der an zwei seiner Fassaden geschlossen ist, um die Öffnung Richtung Nachbargrundstücke zu vermeiden.Die Hülle des Würfels besteht aus Kunststoffmembranen: EPDM für das Dach und PVC mit weißer Teflonausführung für die Fassaden. Der Bau dauerte neun Monate.

Deze kubus van 108 m² met een terras van 31 m² heeft een vierkante plattegrond (12 x 12 m) die aan twee gevels gesloten is ter voorkoming van blootstelling aan belendende percelen. De omtrek van de kubus bestaat uit synthetische membranen: EPDM voor het dak en pvc met witte teflon voor de gevels. De bouw duurde negen maanden.

Este cubo, de 108 m² y una terraza de 31 m², dispone de una planta cuadrada (12 x 12 m) cerrada en dos de sus fachadas para evitar la exposición a las parcelas vecinas. La envolvente del cubo está formada por membranas sintéticas: EPDM para la cubierta y PVC con acabado de teflón blanco para las fachadas. La construcción duró nueve meses.

Questo cubo, di 108 m² con una terrazza di 31 m², presenta una pianta quadrata (12 x 12 m) chiusa su due lati per garantire la riservatezza. Il rivestimento esterno del cubo è formato da membrane sintetiche: EPDM per il tetto e PVC con finitura in teflon bianco per le facciate. La costruzione è durata nove mesi.

Este cubo, de 108 m² com um terraço de 31 m², apresenta uma planta quadrada (12 x 12 m) fechada em duas das suas fachadas para evitar a exposição às parcelas vizinhas. O revestimento do cubo é feito por membranas sintéticas: EPDM para a cobertura e PVC com acabamento de teflon branco para as fachadas. A construção durou nove meses.

Denna kub, som är 108 m² och har en terrass på 31 m², har en kvadratisk planlösning (12 x 12 m) som är stängd vid två av dess fasader för att undvika exponering mot granntomterna. Syntetiska membraner omsluter kuben: EPDM på taket och PVC med finish i vitt teflon på väggarna. Byggnadsarbetet tog nio månader.

North elevation

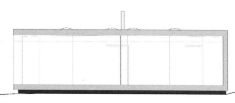

South elevation

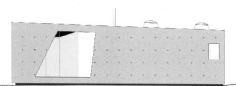

East elevation

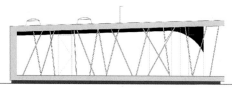

West elevation

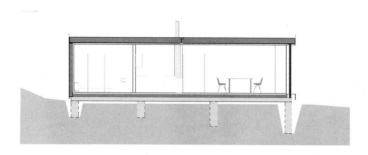

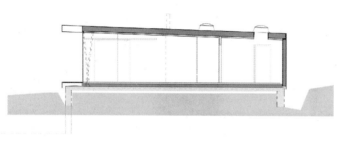

Sections

Floor plan

HIDDEN VALLEY HOUSE

Marmol Radziner Prefab
Moab, UT, USA
© Joe Fletcher

The T-shaped plan house consists of 12 modules with recycled steel profiles and three more modules for the garage. The adaptable spaces open to the outside through the use of glass panes in most of the façades. The construction took seven months, three of which were at the factory.

Cette habitation, avec une base en forme de T, est constituée de douze modules avec des profilés en acier recyclé et de trois modules de plus pour le garage. Des espaces flexibles s'ouvrent sur l'extérieur grâce à l'installation de pans de verre sur la plupart des façades. La construction a duré sept mois, dont trois ont eu lieu en usine.

Das Haus in T-Form setzt sich aus zwölf Modulen mit Recyclingstahlprofilen und drei weiteren Modulen für die Garage zusammen. Die flexiblen Räume öffnen sich dank des Einsatzes von Glaswänden an den meisten Fassaden nach außen hin. Der Bau dauerte sieben Monaten, von denen drei im Werk erfolgten.

Deze woning met plattegrond in T-vorm bestaat uit twaalf modulen met profielen van gerecycled staal, en nog drie voor de garage. De flexibele ruimten zijn naar buiten toe open dankzij glazen panelen in de meeste gevels. De bouw duurde zeven maanden, waarvan drie in de fabriek.

La vivienda, con planta en forma de T, está compuesta por 12 módulos con perfiles de acero reciclado y tres módulos más para el garaje. Los flexibles espacios se abren al exterior gracias al uso de paños de vidrio en la mayoría de las fachadas. La construcción duró siete meses, tres de los cuales fueron en fábrica.

La casa, con pianta a forma di T, si compone di dodici moduli con profili in acciaio riciclato e altri tre moduli per il garage. Gli spazi flessibili si aprono verso l'esterno attraverso l'uso di lastre di vetro nella maggior parte delle facciate. La costruzione è durata sette mesi, tre dei quali in fabbrica.

A casa, com planta em forma de T, é composta por doze módulos com perfis de aço reciclado e três módulos mais para a garagem. Os flexíveis espaços abrem-se para o exterior graças à utilização de cortinas de vidro na maioria das fachadas. A construção durou sete meses, três dos quais foram em fábrica.

Bostaden, som har en T-formad planlösning, består av tolv moduler med profiler av återvunnet stål och ytterligare tre moduler för garaget. De flexibla ytorna vetter mot utomhusmiljön tack vare användning av glaset som finns på de flesta av fasaderna. Byggnadsarbetet tog sju månader, varav tre månader på fabriken.

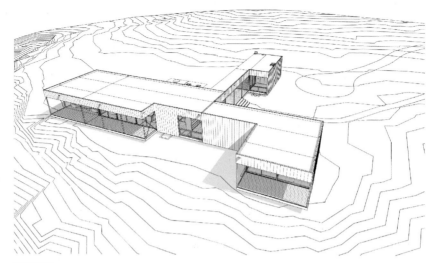

Perspective map

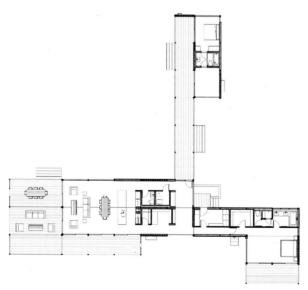

Floor plan

KYOTO HOUSE

Pich-Aguilera
Torre Serona, Spain
© Jordi V. Pou

This 254 m² (2,734 sq ft) house is an example of how to reduce energy demand during construction and the lifetime of a building. The house has devices harnessing solar thermal, photovoltaic and geothermal energy. The entire structure is made of prefabricated concrete panels. Construction time was eight months.

Cette habitation de 254 m² montre comment il est possible de réduire le besoin en énergie pendant la construction et la vie utile d'un bâtiment. Celle-ci est équipée de dispositifs de valorisation de l'énergie solaire thermique, photovoltaïque et géothermique. L'ensemble de la structure a été réalisée avec des panneaux en béton préfabriqués. L'habitation a été construite en huit mois.

Dieses 254 m² große Haus ist ein Beispiel dafür, wie man den Strombedarf während des Baus und der Lebensdauer eines Gebäudes reduzieren kann. Das Haus ist ausgestattet, um Solarthermie-, Fotovoltaik- und Erdwärmeenergie nutzen zu können. Die gesamte Struktur ist aus Fertigbetonpaneelen erstellt. Die Bauzeit betrug acht Monate.

Deze woning van 254 m² is een voorbeeld van hoe het energieverbruik tijdens de bouw en het gebruik van een huis omlaag gebracht kan worden. Het huis beschikt over een systeem voor thermische en fotovoltaïsche zonne-energie en geothermische energie. De hele constructie bestaat uit geprefabriceerde betonnen panelen. De bouw duurde acht maanden.

Esta vivienda de 254 m² es un ejemplo de cómo reducir la demanda energética durante la construcción y la vida útil de un edificio. La casa cuenta con dispositivos de aprovechamiento de energía solar térmica, fotovoltaica y geotérmica. Toda la estructura se realiza con paneles de hormigón prefabricados. El tiempo de construcción fue de ocho meses.

Questa abitazione di 254 m² è un esempio di come ridurre la domanda di energia durante la costruzione e la vita utile di un edificio. La casa è dotata di dispositivi che sfruttano l'energia solare termica, fotovoltaica e geotermica. L'intera struttura è composta da pannelli prefabbricati in calcestruzzo. Il periodo di costruzione è stato di otto mesi.

Esta casa de 254 m² é um exemplo de como reduzir a demanda energética durante a construção e vida útil de um edifício. A casa conta com dispositivos de aproveitamento de energia solar térmica, fotovoltaica e geotérmica. Toda a estrutura é feita com painéis de betão pré-fabricados. O tempo de construção foi de oito meses.

Denna bostad på 254 m² är ett exempel på hur man kan minska energibehovet under en byggnads uppförande och livslängd. Huset har apparater som utnyttjar den termiska, fotovoltaiska och geotermiska solenergin. Hela stommen är gjord av monteringsfärdiga paneler av betong. Byggnadsarbetet tog åtta månader.

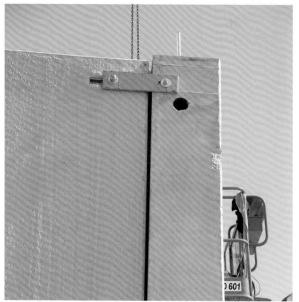

Second floor

Roof

Ground floor

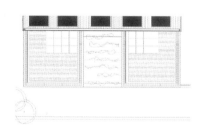

Basement

RESIDENCE FOR A **SCULPTOR**

Sander Architects
Santa Rosa, CA, USA
© Sharon Risedorph Photography

This program consists of a 418 m² (4,499 sq ft) house distributed over two floors with three bedrooms and a studio-workshop for a sculptor. The use of a lightweight prefabricated structure has allowed the house to be customized. The prefabrication system used, apart from generating less waste, has also managed to reduce the final cost of the work to about 1,590 euros/m².

Ce projet consiste en une habitation de 418 m² à deux étages, avec trois chambres et un studio-atelier pour un sculpteur. L'utilisation d'une structure légère préfabriquée donne de la personnalité à la maison. Le système de préfabrication employé produit non seulement moins de déchets, mais a également permis de réduire le coût final des travaux d'environ 1 590 euros/m².

Dieses Programm umfasst ein 418 m² großes Haus auf zwei Stockwerken, mit drei Schlafzimmern und einem großen Bildhauerstudio / Werkstatt. Durch die Verwendung einer leichten Fertigstruktur konnte das Haus persönlich angepasst werden. Das eingesetzte Fertigbausystem machte es möglich, die Bauenkosten auf rund 1.590,- Euro / m² zu reduzieren – abgesehen von der Tatsache, dass weniger Abfälle erzeugt werden.

Dit project bestaat uit een woning van 418 m² van twee verdiepingen met drie slaapkamers en een atelier voor een beeldhouwer. Door een lichte prefabconstructie te kiezen kon de woning toch een persoonlijke touch krijgen. Het gebruikte prefabsysteem drukte niet alleen de kosten, die uitkwamen op 1590 euro/m², maar genereerde tevens minder afval.

Este programa consiste en una vivienda de 418 m² de dos plantas con tres dormitorios y un estudio-taller para un escultor. El uso de una ligera estructura prefabricada ha permitido personalizar la casa. El sistema de prefabricación empleado, aparte de generar menos residuos, también ha conseguido reducir el coste final de la obra a unos 1.590 euros/m².

Questo programma comprende un'abitazione di 418 m² su due piani con tre stanze da letto e uno studio-atelier per uno scultore. L'uso di una struttura prefabbricata leggera ha consentito di personalizzare la casa. Il sistema di prefabbricazione utilizzato, oltre a generare meno rifiuti, è anche riuscito a ridurre il costo finale dell'opera a circa 1.590 euro/m².

Este programa consiste numa casa de 418 m² de dois pisos com três quartos e um atelier para um escultor. A utilização de uma leve estrutura pré-fabricada permitiu personalizar a casa. O sistema de prefabricação empregue, aparte de gerar menos resíduos, também conseguiu reduzir o custo final da obra para cerca de 1.590 euros/m².

Detta program består av en bostad på 418 m² med två våningar med tre sovrum och en studio-verkstad för en skulptör. Användning av en enkel monteringsfärdig stomme har gjort det möjligt att göra huset personligt. Det monteringsfärdiga systemet som har använts, förutom att det genererar mindre avfall, har dessutom lett till att den slutliga kostnaden för byggnadsarbetet har minskat till cirka 1.590 euros/m².

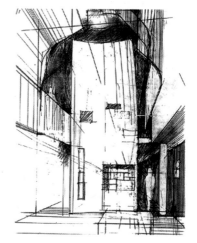

Sketches

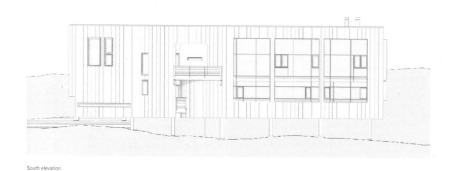

South elevation

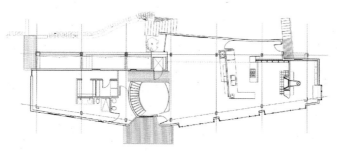

Second floor

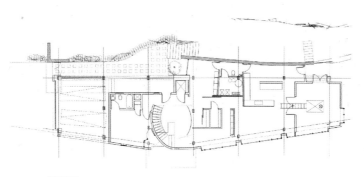

Ground floor

SYSTEM3

Oskar Leo Kaufmann, Albert Rüf
MoMA, New York, NY, USA
© Adolf Bereuter

For the exhibition Home Delivery: Fabricating the Modern Dwelling, held in summer 2008 at the MoMA and dedicated to prefabrication and modular systems, the Austrian studio presented System3, an ideal prototype of transportable, expandable and durable housing. The basic module is 53 m² (570 sq ft).

À l'occasion de l'exposition *Home Delivery: Fabricating the Modern Dwelling*, organisée par le MoMA en été 2008 et consacrée à la préfabrication et aux systèmes modulaires, le studio autrichien a présenté System3, un prototype idéal d'habitation transportable, extensible et durable. Le module de base a une surface de 53 m².

Für die im Sommer 2008 im MoMA veranstaltete *Home Delivery: Fabricating the Modern Dwelling* Ausstellung von Fertigbau- und Modularsystemen stellte das österreichische Atelier System3 vor. Dabei handelt es um einen idealen Prototypen eines transportierbaren, erweiterbaren und dauerhaften Hauses. Die Basismodulfläche beträgt 53 m².

Voor de expositie 'Home Delivery: Fabricating the Modern Dwelling', die in de zomer van 2008 in het MoMA werd gehouden en was gewijd aan prefabricage en modulaire systemen, toonde de oostenrijkse studio System3 een ideaal prototype van een vervoerbare, uitbreidbare en duurzame woning. De basismodule heeft een oppervlakte van 53 m².

Para la exposición «Home Delivery: Fabricating the Modern Dwelling», celebrada en verano de 2008 en el MoMA y dedicada a la prefabricación y los sistemas modulares, el estudio austriaco presentó System3, un prototipo ideal de vivienda transportable, expandible y duradera. El módulo básico mide 53 m² de superficie.

Per l'esposizione *Home Delivery: Fabricating the Modern Dwelling*, ospitata nell'estate del 2008 dal MoMA e dedicata alla prefabbricazione e ai sistemi modulari, lo studio austriaco ha presentato System3, un prototipo ideale di abitazione trasportabile, espandibile e durevole. Il modulo di base misura 53 m² di superficie.

Para a exposição *Home Delivery: Fabricating the Modern Dwelling*, realizada no verão de 2008 no MoMA e dedicada à prefabricação e aos sistemas modulares, o estúdio austríaco apresentou System3, um protótipo ideal de casa transportável, expansível e duradoura. O módulo básico mede 53 m² de superfície.

För utställningen *Home Delivery: Fabricating the Modern Dwelling*, som ägde rum sommaren 2008 i MoMA och som ägnades åt monteringsfärdiga modulära system, presenterade den österrikiska studion System3, en prototyp som är idealisk för den transporterbara, expanderbara och varaktiga bostaden. Basmodulen har en yta på 53 m².

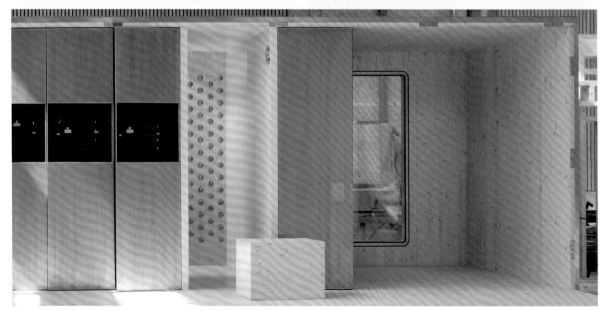

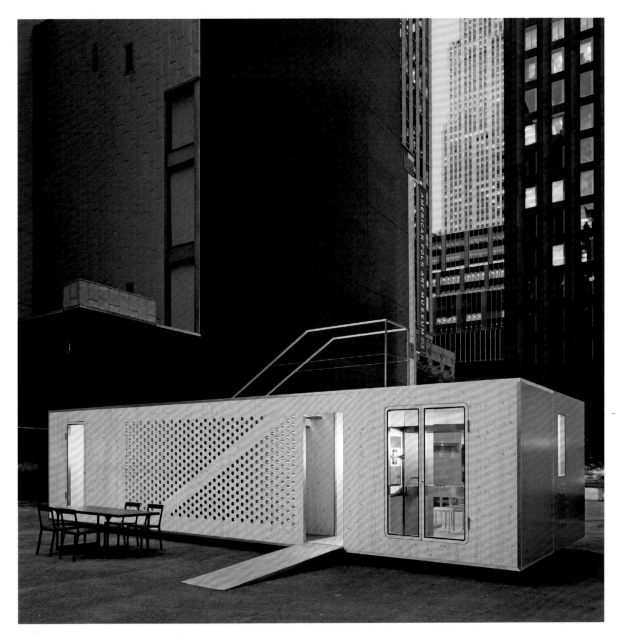

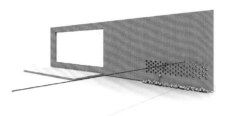

Axonometric view

Deconstructed axonometric view

CNC technology – process

CNC technology – finished

Coating

Window

Model 2008 (53 m²/570 sq ft) – living area, bedroom, kitchen, bath and roof deck

Model 2010 (86 m²/926 sq ft) – expanded living area, bedroom, kitchen, bath and roof deck

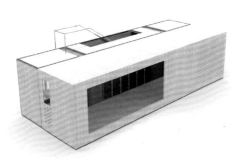

Model 2016 (140 m²/1,496 sq ft) – expanded living area, kitchen, bath for guests, master bedroom with bath, bedroom with bath, roofed frontyard/carport and two roof decks

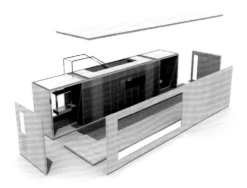

Model 2028 (159 m²/1,711 sq ft) – living area, kitchen, bath for guests, master bedroom with bath, bedroom with bath, studio with bath and kitchen on the third floor, roofed frontyard/carport and three roof decks

PARASITE **LAS PALMAS**

Korteknie Stuhlmacher Architecten
Rotterdam, The Netherlands
© Anne Bousema

Located in Rotterdam, Parasite Las Palmas became a pilot project. It is based on a small building that grew as a parasite in a suburban area. Like a real scale model, the prototype explores the technological advantages of prefabrication.

Situé à Rotterdam, Parasite Las Palmas est devenu un projet expérimental, basé sur une petite construction, qui a grandi tel un parasite dans un espace suburbain. Le prototype, telle une maquette à échelle réelle, explore les avantages technologiques de la préfabrication.

Parasite Las Palmas in Rotterdam hat sich in ein Versuchsprojekt verwandelt. Das Projekt basiert auf einem kleinen Gebäude, das innerhalb eines Vorstadtgebiets wie ein Parasit gewachsen ist. Wie eine Nachbildung aber in Istgröße erkundet der Prototyp die technologischen Vorteile des Fertigbaus.

Parasite Las Palmas in Rotterdam veranderde in een experimenteel project dat is gebaseerd op de bouw van een kleine constructie die als een parasiet uitgroeide in een voorstedelijke ruimte. Als een maquette op werkelijke schaal verkent het prototype de technologische voordelen van prefabricage.

Situado en Róterdam, Parasite Las Palmas se convirtió en un proyecto experimental. Se basa en una pequeña construcción que creció como un parásito en un espacio suburbano. Como si fuera una maqueta a escala real, el prototipo explora las ventajas tecnológicas de la prefabricación.

Ubicato a Rotterdam, Parasite Las Palmas è diventato un progetto sperimentale. Il progetto si basa su un piccolo edificio che è cresciuto come un parassita in una zona suburbana. Come un vero e proprio prototipo a dimensione naturale esplora i vantaggi tecnologici della prefabbricazione.

Situado em Roterdão, Parasite Las Palmas converteu-se num projecto experimental. O projecto baseia-se numa pequena construção que cresceu como um parasita, num espaço suburbano. Como se fosse uma maqueta à escala real, o protótipo explora as vantagens tecnológicas da prefabricação.

Parasite Las Palmas, som ligger i Rotterdam, har blivit ett projekt för experiment. Projektet baserades på en liten konstruktion som växte som en parasit, i ett förortsområde. Som om den vore en dummy i verklig storlek, utforskar modellen de tekniska fördelarna med monteringsfärdiga lösningar.

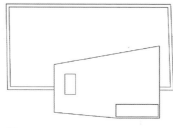

Roof

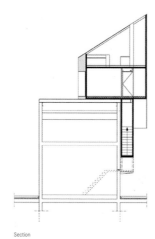

Section

LAIDLEY STREET RESIDENCE

Zach/de Vito Architecture
San Francisco, CA, USA
© Zach/de Vito Architecture

This home is an example of how to create a modern prefab, sustainable and urban house. The open plan comprises two lateral volumes. The larger volume is composed of three levels. The shorter volume offers views to the south and benefits from light. Steel and wood materials are the most predominant materials.

Cette habitation est l'exemple même d'une maison préfabriquée moderne, durable et urbaine. L'espace ouvert est composé de deux volumes latéraux. Le volume le plus grand se répartit sur trois niveaux, alors que le plus petit donne sur le sud et bénéficie d'une bonne luminosité. L'acier et le bois sont les matériaux dominants.

Dieses Haus ist ein Beispiel dafür, wie man ein modernes, nachhaltiges und städtisches Fertighaus bauen kann. Der offene Grundriss umfasst zwei seitliche Volumen. Das größte Volumen besteht aus drei Ebenen. Das kürzeste Volumen ermöglicht Ausblicke Richtung Süden und nützt das Licht. Stahl und Holz sind die vorherrschenden Baustoffe.

Deze woning is een typisch voorbeeld van een modern, duurzaam, stedelijk prefabhuis. De open plattegrond bestaat uit twee naast elkaar gelegen delen. Het grootste deel heeft drie niveaus. Het korste deel biedt uitzicht op het zuiden en profiteert van het licht. Als materialen zijn voornamelijk staal en hout gebruikt.

Esta vivienda es un ejemplo de cómo crear una casa prefabricada moderna, sostenible y urbana. El plano abierto se compone de dos volúmenes laterales. El volumen más grande se compone de tres niveles. El volumen más corto permite vistas hacia el sur y se beneficia de la luz. El acero y la madera se imponen como materiales predominantes.

Questa abitazione è un esempio di come creare un prefabbricato moderno, sostenibile e urbano. Il piano aperto comprende due volumi laterali. Il volume principale è composto da tre livelli. Il volume più corto è rivolto a sud e riceve molta luce naturale. L'acciaio e il legno si sono imposti come materiali predominanti.

Esta casa é um exemplo de como criar uma casa pré-fabricada moderna, sustentável e urbana. O espaço aberto engloba dois volumes laterais. O volume maior é composto por três níveis. O volume mais curto oferece vista para o sul e beneficia da luz. O aço e a madeira são os materiais mais predominantes.

Denna bostad är ett exempel på hur man skapar ett modernt och urbant monteringsfärdigt hus som är ekologiskt hållbart. Den öppna planlösningen består av två sidovolymer. Den största volymen består av tre nivåer. Den kortaste volymen har utsikt mot söder och tar tillvara på ljuset. Stål och trä är de dominerande materialen.

Digital model used for fabrication

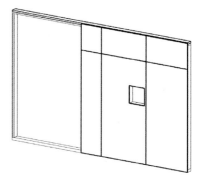

Exterior wall panel 1-6

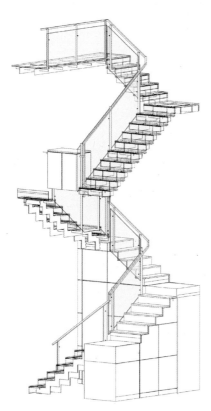

Axonometric view of the stair

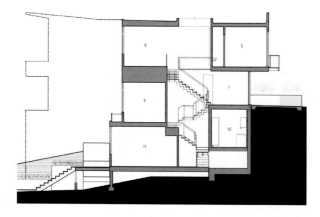

1.	Entry	8.	Living room
2.	Garage	9.	Sitting room
3.	Master suite	10.	Family room
4.	Bathroom	11.	Bedroom
5.	Guest room	12.	Laundry
6.	Kitchen	13.	Mechanical room
7.	Dining room	14.	Deck

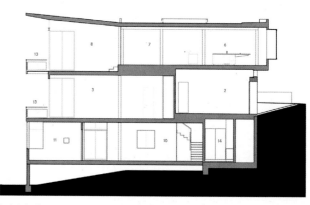

Longitudinal sections

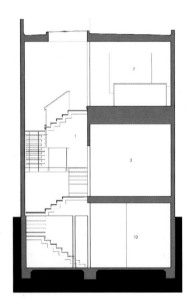

Transverse section

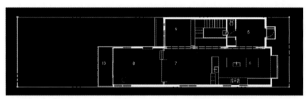

Second floor

Ground floor

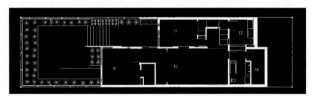

Basement

1.	Entry	8.	Living room
2.	Garage	9.	Sitting room
3.	Master suite	10.	Family room
4.	Bathroom	11.	Bedroom
5.	Guest room	12.	Laundry
6.	Kitchen	13.	Deck
7.	Dining room	14.	Mechanical room

STRECKHOF RELOADED

Franz Architekten
Zellerndorf, Austria
© Lisa Rastl

This house in Zellerndorf, Austria consists of three separate units connected by a glass corridor. The three volumes house different functions: the garage in the area closest to the street, the daytime areas in the center, and bedrooms in the most private unit.

Cette maison située à Zellerndorf, en Autriche, est composée de trois unités indépendantes, reliées entre elles par un couloir de verre. Les trois volumes remplissent des fonctions différentes : le garage se trouve à proximité de la rue, les salles de séjour au centre et les chambres dans la zone la plus intime.

Das in Zellerndorf, Österreich, gelegene Haus umfasst drei eigenständige Einheiten, die durch einen Glaskorridor verbunden sind. Die drei Volumina beinhalten unterschiedliche Funktionen, wobei die Garage am nächsten and der Straße, die Bereiche für den Tag in der Mitte und die Schlafzimmer im privaten Bereich liegen.

Dit huis in Zellerndorf, Oostenrijk, bestaat uit drie aparte delen die met elkaar zijn verbonden met een glazen gang. De drie delen hebben verschillende functies: de garage bevindt zich in het deel het dichtst bij de straat, de leefruimten bevinden zich in het midden en de slaapkamers in het meest afgescheiden deel.

Esta casa situada, en Zellerndorf (Austria), se compone de tres unidades independientes unidas por un corredor de cristal. Los tres volúmenes albergan funciones distintas: el garaje en la zona más próxima a la calle, las zonas de día en el centro, y los dormitorios en la unidad más privada.

Questa casa che si trova a Zellerndorf, in Austria, è costituita da tre unità indipendenti collegate da un corridoio di vetro. I tre volumi assolvono a funzioni diverse, il garage nella zona più vicina alla strada, le aree diurne al centro e le camere da letto nell'unità più interna.

Esta casa em Zellerndorf, Áustria, consiste em três unidades independentes ligadas por um corredor de vidro. Os três volumes albergam diferentes funções, a garagem na área mais próxima da rua, as áreas diurnas no centro, e os quartos na unidade mais privada.

Det här huset som ligger i Zellendorf, Österrike, består av tre oberoende enheter som är förenade av en glaskorridor. De tre volymerna har olika funktioner: garaget ligger i området närmast gatan, ytorna som används dagtid i centrum och sovrummen i den mest privata delen.

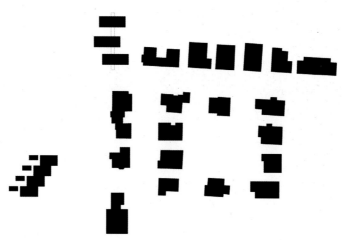

Site plan

Elevation

Longitudinal section

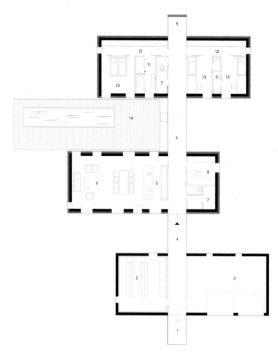

1. Entry
2. Workshop
3. Garage
4. Hallway
5. Kitchen
6. Dining room/living room
7. Technical system
8. Study
9. Reading alcove
10. Bedroom
11. Bathroom
12. Walk-in closet
13. Child room
14. Terrace/pool

THE **NUMBER** HOUSE

Mitsutomo Matsunami Architect & Associates
Hozumidai, Japan
© Mitsutomo Matsunami Architect & Associates

This row of prefabricated houses is characterized by a façade that looks like a sequence of numbers. The four façades appear as if they were one.

Cette rangée de maisons préfabriquées se caractérise par les quatre façades, qui semblent former une série de nombres reliés entre eux.

Diese Fertighäuserreihe kennzeichnet durch eine Fassade, die wie eine Reihenfolge an Zahlen aussieht. Die vier Fassaden sehen wir nur eine aus.

Deze rij prefabhuizen wordt gekenmerkt door een voorgevel die op een reeks getallen lijkt. De vier gevels lijken samen een.

Esta hilera de casas prefabricadas se caracteriza por una fachada que parece una secuencia de números. Las cuatro fachadas aparecen como si fueran una sola.

Questa schiera di case prefabbricate è caratterizzata da una facciata che sembra una sequenza di numeri. Le quattro facciate appaiono come se fossero una sola.

Esta fileira de casas pré-fabricadas caracteriza-se por uma fachada que parece uma sequência de números. As quatro fachadas aparentam ser apenas uma.

Denna länga med monteringsfärdiga hus kännetecknas av en fasad som verkar vara en sekvens av nummer. De fyra fasaderna framträder som om de endast vore en.

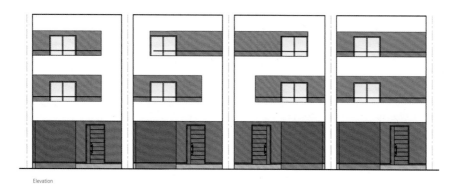

Elevation

Floor plans

A-RING HOUSE

Atelier Tekuto
Kanazawa, Japan
© Toshihiro Sobajima

This house with aluminum frame is designed to function as a large radiator. The house uses the power of geothermal energy and other active systems, such as solar panels, a roof garden or rainwater collection systems.

Cette maison, avec une structure en aluminium, a été conçue pour fonctionner comme un grand radiateur. En effet, cette habitation utilise l'énergie géothermique et d'autres systèmes actifs tels que des panneaux solaires, une toiture végétale ou des systèmes de récupération des eaux pluviales.

Dieses Haus mit Aluminiumstruktur soll wie ein großer Heizkörper funktionieren. Es wird mit Erdwärme beheizt und bedient sich weiterer aktiver Systeme wie Solarplatten, einem begrünten Dach oder Regenwasserauffangvorrichtungen.

De bedoeling van dit huis met aluminium skelet is dat het werkt al seen grote radiator. Het huis maakt gebruik van geothermische energie (aardwarmte) en andere actieve systemen, zoals zonnepanelen, een groen dak of regenwatersystemen.

Esta casa con estructura de aluminio está pensada para que funcione como un gran radiador. La vivienda se vale del poder de la energía geotérmica y otros sistemas activos, como placas solares, una cubierta ajardinada o sistemas de recogidas de aguas pluviales.

Questa casa con struttura in alluminio è stata progettata per funzionare come un enorme radiatore. La casa utilizza l'energia geotermica e altri sistemi attivi quali i pannelli solari, un giardino pensile e sistemi di raccolta dell'acqua piovana.

Esta casa com estrutura de alumínio é concebida para funcionar como um grande radiador. A casa utiliza energia geotérmica e outros sistemas activos como painéis solares, um jardim no telhado ou sistemas de captação de águas pluviais.

Detta hus med aluminiumstomme är tänkt att det ska fungera som ett stort värmeelement. Bostaden tar vara på den geotermiska energin och andra aktiva system som solfångare, ett skyddstak med planteringar eller system för insamling av regnvatten.

Section

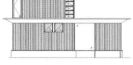

North elevation

East elevation

South elevation

West elevation

Basement

Ground floor

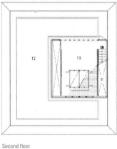

Second floor

1. Entry
2. Living room
3. Kitchen/dining room
4. Garage
5. Store room
6. Toilet
7. Sanitary
8. Green curtains
9. Terrace
10. Bedroom
11. Void
12. Roof garden

QUBIC STUDENT HOUSING UNITS

HVDN Architecten
Amsterdam, The Netherlands
© Luuk Kramer

This student residence is composed of 715 households of small dimensions with a capacity for 1,000 students. The project was constructed in 12 months through the use of prefabricated units as containers, creating a façade of different colors.

Cette résidence universitaire est constituée de 715 habitations de taille réduite, avec une capacité d'accueil de 1 000 étudiants. Le projet a été réalisé en un an, grâce à l'utilisation d'unités préfabriquées de type containers, qui forment une façade de différentes couleurs.

Dieses Studentenwohnheim besteht aus 715 Wohnungen mit kleinen Abmessungen und bietet 1.000 Studenten Platz. Das Projekt wurde in zwölf Monaten dank der Verwendung von Fertigeinheiten in der Art von Containern erbaut, wobei eine Fassade mit unterschiedlichen Farben entstand.

Dit studentencomplex bestaat uit 715 bescheiden woningen en kan 1000 studenten huisvesten. Het werd in 12 maanden gebouwd dankzij de toepassing van prefabeenheden in containerformaat. De gevel heeft verschillende kleuren.

Esta residencia de estudiantes se compone de 715 viviendas de reducidas dimensiones con una capacidad para 1.000 estudiantes. El proyecto fue construido en 12 meses gracias a la utilización de unidades prefabricadas a modo de contenedores, creando una fachada de diferentes colores.

Questo residence per studenti è composto da 715 abitazioni di dimensioni ridotte con una capacità per 1000 studenti. Il progetto è stato costruito in dodici mesi mediante l'uso di unità prefabbricate come container, creando una facciata multicolore.

Esta residência estudantil é composta por 715 apartamentos de dimensões reduzidas com uma capacidade para 1000 estudantes. O projecto foi construído em doze meses graças à utilização de unidades pré-fabricadas como contentores, criando uma fachada de diferentes cores.

Detta studentresidens har plats för 1000 studenter och består av 715 bostäder i små dimensioner. Projektet byggdes på tolv månader tack vare att monteringsfärdiga enheter i containerform användes och en fasad i olika färger skapades.

North façade

South façade

West façade

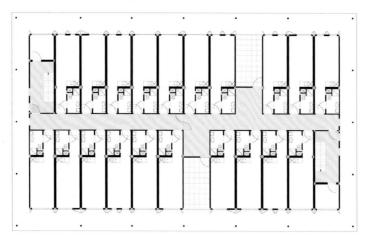

Second floor

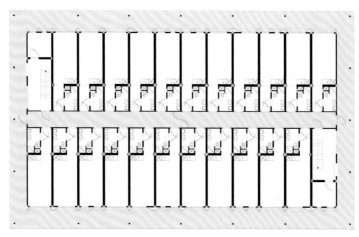

Ground floor

HOUSE N° 19

Korteknie Stuhlmacher Architecten, BikvanderPol artists
Utrecht, The Netherlands
© Christian Kahl, Korteknie Stuhlmacher Architecten

This project was supported by the SEV, within its IFD program. SEV stands for The Steering Committee for Experiments in Public Housing, an independent organization in The Netherlands that financially supports any initiatives related to construction. The model is 100% prefabricated.

Ce projet a été subventionné par le SEV, dans le cadre de son programme IFD. Les sigles SEV font référence à The Steering Committee for Experiments in Public Housing, une organisation indépendante hollandaise, qui soutient économiquement des initiatives dans le domaine de la construction. Le prototype est 100 % préfabriqué.

Dieses Projekt wurde von SEV innerhalb seines IFD-Programms unterstützt. Die Abkürzung SEV steht für The Steering Committee for Experiments in Public Housing, einer eigenständigen Organisation in Holland, die bestimmte Initiativen im Zusammenhang mit dem Bauwesen unterstützt. Hierbei handelt es sich um ein 100 %-ges Fertighausmodell.

Dit project werd gesubsidieerd door het SEV-programma IFD-bouwen. De afkorting SEV staat voor Stuurgroep Experimenten Volkshuisvesting, een onafhankelijke Nederlandse organisatie die bepaalde bouwprojecten financieel ondersteunt. Het model is 100% prefab.

Este proyecto fue subvencionado por el SEV, dentro de su programa IFD. Las siglas del SEV aluden a The Steering Committee for Experiments in Public Housing, una organización independiente de los Países Bajos que apoya económicamente alguna iniciativas relacionadas con la construcción. El modelo es 100% prefabricado.

Questo progetto è stato finanziato dal SEV, nell'ambito del suo programma IFD. Le sigle del SEV alludono a The Steering Committee for Experiments in Public Housing, un'organizzazione olandese indipendente che sostiene economicamente alcune iniziative relative alla costruzione. Il modello è prefabbricato al 100%.

Este projecto foi subsidiado pelo SEV, dentro do seu programa IFD. SEV significa The Steering Committee for Experiments in Public, uma organização independente na Holanda que apoia financeiramente qualquer iniciativa relacionada com a construção. O modelo é 100% pré-fabricado.

Detta projekt subventionerades av SEV, inom dess IFD-program. Akronymen SEV syftar på The Steering Committee for Experiments in Public Housing, en oberoende organisation i Holland som ger ekonomiskt stöd till en del initiativ som har samband med byggsektorn. Modellen är 100 % monteringsfärdig.

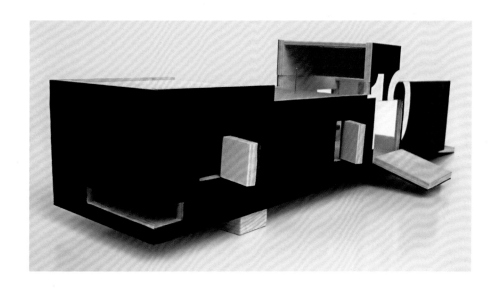

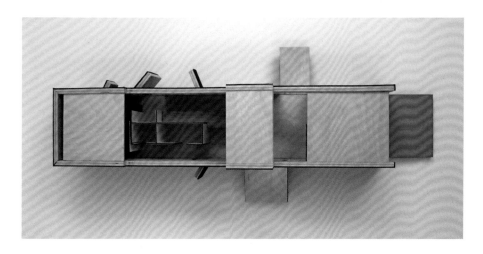

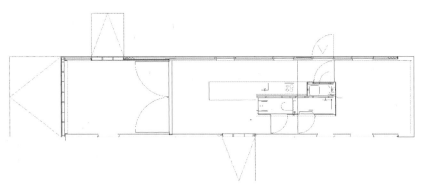

Floor plan

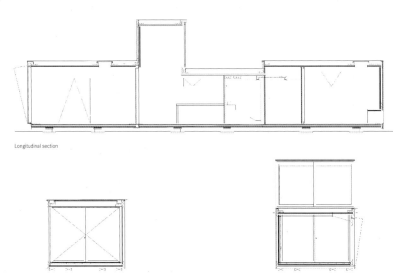

Longitudinal section

Transversal sections

REDONDO BEACH HOUSE

DeMaria Design Associates
Redondo Beach, CA, USA
© Andre Movsesyan, Christian Kienapfel

The structure of this home located in a suburban area near Los Angeles is based on the figure of a Cargo-type ISO container type, 12 m (40 ft) in length. The reuse of eight of these containers generates a flexible housing structure. The energy consumed during construction is 400 kWh/container.

La structure de cette habitation, située dans la banlieue de Los Angeles, est basée sur le modèle d'un container ISO de type Cargo de 12 m de longueur. La réutilisation de 8 de ces conteneurs crée une structure habitable flexible. L'énergie consommée pendant la construction a été de 400 kWh par container.

Die Struktur dieser Wohnung, die sich in einem Vorort in der Nähe von Los Angeles befindet, basiert auf der eines 12 m langen ISO-Frachtcontainers. Die Wiederverwendung von 8 dieser Container bildet die Struktur eines flexiblen Hauses. Die während des Baus verbrauchte Energie betrug 400 kWh/Container.

De structuur van deze woning in een buitenwijk nabij Los Angeles is gebaseerd op de vorm van een ISO-container type Cargo van 12 meter lang. Het hergebruik van acht van dit soort containers biedt de mogelijk tot het creëren van een flexibele woning. De energie die wordt verbruikt tijdens de bouw is 400 kWh/container.

La estructura de esta vivienda situada en una zona residencial cerca de Los Ángeles está basada en la figura de un container ISO del tipo Cargo de 12 m de longitud. La reutilización de ocho de estos contenedores genera una estructura de vivienda flexible. La energía consumida durante la construcción es de 400 kWh por contenedor.

La struttura di questa abitazione situata in una zona periferica nei pressi di Los Angeles è basata sulla figura di un container ISO tipo Cargo di 12 m di lunghezza. Il riutilizzo di 8 di questi container genera una struttura abitativa flessibile. L'energia consumata durante la costruzione è di 400 kWh/container.

A estrutura desta casa localizada numa área suburbana perto de Los Angeles é baseada na aparência de contentor ISO do tipo Cargo de 12 m/40 ft de comprimento. A reutilização de oito destes contentores gera uma estrutura flexível de alojamento. A energia consumida durante a construção é 400 kWh/contentor.

Strukturen på denna bostad, som ligger i ett förortsområde nära Los Angeles, baseras på figuren av en ISO-container av typen Cargo som är 12 m lång. Återanvändningen av 8 av dessa containrar skapar en stomme som ger en flexibel bostad. Energin som förbrukas under byggnationen är 400 kWh/container.

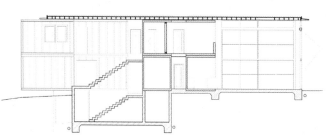

Longitudinal section

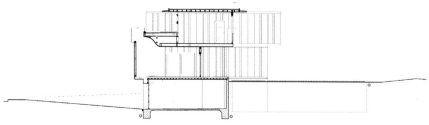

Transversal section

North elevation

South elevation

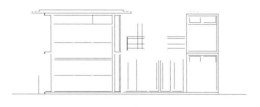

East elevation

West elevation

Second floor

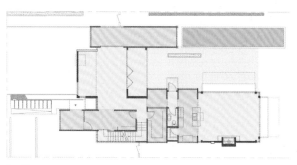

Ground floor

Basement

SUSTAINABLE PROTOTYPE

Studio 804 (University of Kansas, School of Architecture and Urban Planning)
Greensburg, KS, USA
© Courtesy of Studio 804

The construction and delivery of the Sustainable Prototype was conducted one year after a tornado devastated the Greensburg area. The main environmental strategies of the prototype were the use of active and passive systems in pursuit of good bioclimatic principles, the use of recycled materials, and their respectful implementation into the area.

La construction et la livraison du Prototype Durable ont été effectuées un an après le passage d'une tornade, qui a dévasté la zone de Greensburg. Les principales stratégies environnementales mises en place dans ce prototype ont été l'utilisation de systèmes actifs et passifs en vue de créer un espace bioclimatique optimal, l'utilisation de matériaux recyclés et un emplacement respectueux de son environnement.

Bau und Lieferung des nachhaltigen Prototypen erfolgten ein Jahr nachdem ein Tornado das Gebiet von Greensburg verwüstet hatte. Die wichtigsten umweltschützenden Strategien des Prototypen waren der Einsatz aktiver und passiver Systeme für ein gutes Bioklima, die Verwendung recycelten Baumaterials und der respektvolle Einbau auf dem Gelände.

De bouw en oplevering van dit Duurzame Prototype vonden plaats een jaar nadat een tornado zijn verwoestende werking had gedaan in de omgeving van Greensburg. De belangrijkste strategieën op milieugebied van dit prototype waren het gebruik van actieve en passieve systemen ten behoeve van een goed bioklimaat, het gebruik van gerecyclede materialen en de plaatsing met respect voor de omgeving.

La construcción y entrega del Prototipo Sostenible se realizó un año después de que un tornado debastara la zona de Greensburg. Las principales estrategias medioambientales del prototipo fueron la aplicación de sistemas activos y pasivos en pos de una buena bioclimática, el uso de materiales reciclados y una implantación respetuosa en el terreno.

La costruzione e la consegna del Prototipo Sostenibile è avvenuta a un anno di distanza dal passaggio di un tornado che ha devastato la zona di Greensburg. Le strategie di progettazione principali del prototipo sono l'impiego di sistemi attivi e passivi volti a renderlo ecocompatibili, l'uso di materiali riciclati e la costruzione rispettosa del terreno.

A construção e entrega do Protótipo Sustentável realizaram-se um ano após um tornado ter devastado a área de Greensburg. As principais estratégias ambientais do protótipo foram a utilização de sistemas activos e passivos em busca de bons princípios bioclimáticos, a utilização de materiais reciclados, e a sua respeitadora implantação no terreno.

Byggnationen och överlämnandet av den ekologiskt hållbara prototypen gjordes ett år efter det att en tornado ödelade området Greensburg. Prototypens huvudsakliga miljöstrategier var användning av aktiva och passiva system på jakt efter ett bra bioklimat, användning av återvunna material och respektfull placering på tomten.

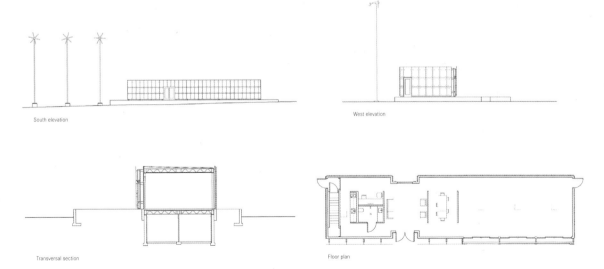

South elevation

West elevation

Transversal section

Floor plan

CAMP **WILDALPEN MOUNTAIN** RESORT

Holzbox
Wildalpen, Austria
© Birgit Koell

This campus, located in a rural setting near the river Salza, has been funded through the Leader Plus project of the European Union and the economic boost from the Government of the province of Styria. This program aims to encourage the development of regional and vernacular architecture. Energy demand to acclimate the building is 49 kWh/m².

Ce campus, situé en zone rurale près du fleuve Salza, a été financé par le projet Leader Plus de l'Union Européenne, ainsi que l'aide économique du Gouvernement de la province de Styria. Ce programme a pour but d'encourager le développement de l'architecture régionale et autochtone. Le besoin en énergie pour acclimater le bâtiment est de 49 kWh/m².

Dieser Campus, der in einer ländlichen Gegend in der Nähe des Salza Flusses liegt, wurde dank des Leader Plus Projekt der Europäischen Union und des wirtschaftlichen Impulses der Regierung der Steiermark finanziert. Das Programm bezweckt, die Entwicklung der regionalen und einheimischen Architektur zu fördern. Der Energiebedarf zur Klimatisierung des Gebäudes beträgt 49 kWh/m².

Deze campus in een landelijke omgeving nabij de rivier de Salza is gefinancieerd door het project Leader Plus van de Europese Unie en de subsudie van de provincie Stiermarken. Genoemd project stelt zich ten doel de regionale en streekeigen architectuur te stimuleren. De energie die benodigd is voor het verwarmen en koelen van het gebouw is 49 kWh/m².

Este campus, situado en un entorno rural cerca del río Salza, ha sido financiado gracias al proyecto Leader Plus de la Unión Europea y al impulso económico del Gobierno de la provincia de Estiria. Dicho programa persigue incentivar el desarrollo de la arquitectura regional y vernácula. La demanda energética para aclimatar el edificio es de 49 kWh/m².

Questo campus, situato in una zona rurale del fiume Salzach, è stato finanziato grazie al progetto Leader Plus dell'Unione Europea e all'impulso economico del governo della Stiria. Questo programma mira a incoraggiare lo sviluppo dell'architettura regionale e locale. Le necessità energetiche della costruzione sono di 49 kWh/m².

Este campus localizado num ambiente rural perto do rio Salza foi financiado através do projecto Leader Plus da União Europeia e do estímulo económico do Governo da província de Styria. Este programa tem como objectivo incentivar o desenvolvimento da arquitectura regional e vernacular. A energia necessária para aclimatizar o edifício é 49 kWh/m².

Detta campus, som ligger i ett jordbruksområde nära floden Salza, har finansierats tack vare EU-projektet Leader Plus och den ekonomiska stimulansen från regeringen i provinsen Styria. Nämnda program söker sporra utvecklingen av den regionala och inhemska arkitekturen. För att värma upp eller kyla ner byggnaden krävs 49 kWh/m².

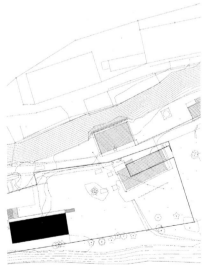

Site plan

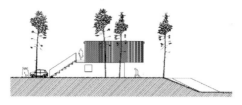

North elevation

Section 1

Section 2

West elevation

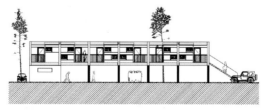

East elevation

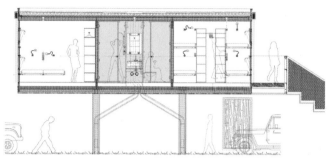

Longitudinal section of module-apartment

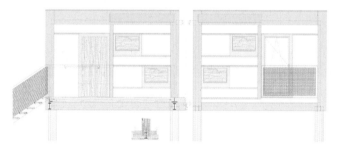

Transversal sections of module-apartment

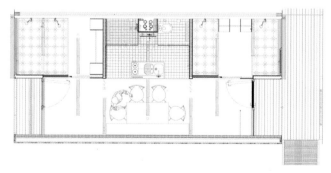

Floor plan of module-apartment

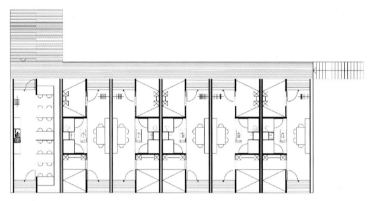

Second floor

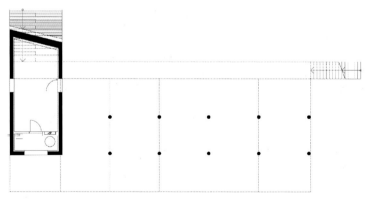

Ground floor

PLATFORM FOR VIEWS OF **VOESTALPINE LINZ**

Caramel architekten ZT, F. Stiper
Linz, Austria
© Caramel architekten

Caramel developed a standard module as a basic element for each platform. The modules are symmetrical in shape and can be combined in a random manner which meets the needs of size and shape desired by the customer. All of them have been built at the factory and suspended in situ.

Caramel a conçu un module standard qui sert d'élément de base à chaque plateforme. Les modules présentent une géométrie symétrique et peuvent être combinés de manière aléatoire, afin de répondre aux besoins du client sur la taille et la forme. Tous ont été fabriqués en usine et installés sur place.

Caramel entwickelte ein Standardmodul als grundlegendes Element für jede Plattform. Die Module sind symmetrisch in ihrer Form und können beliebig kombiniert werden, sodass sie den vom Kunden gewünschten Größen- und Formbedürfnissen entsprechen. Sie wurden alle im Werk hergestellt und vor Ort aufgehängt.

Caramel ontwikkelde een standaardmodule als basiselement voor elk platform. De modulen zijn symmetrisch en kunnen op willekeurige wijze gecombineerd worden naargelang de door de klant gewenste afmetingen en vorm. Alle modulen zijn in de fabriek vervaardigd en ter plekke opgehangen.

Caramel desarrolló un módulo estándar como elemento básico para cada plataforma. Los módulos son simétricos en forma y pueden ser combinados de una manera aleatoria que responda a las necesidades de tamaño y forma deseada por el cliente. Todos ellos han sido construidos en fábrica y suspendidos in situ.

Caramel ha sviluppato un modulo standard come elemento di base per ciascuna piattaforma. I moduli hanno forma simmetrica e possono essere combinati in modo casuale per soddisfare le esigenze di dimensioni e di forma del cliente. Tutti sono stati costruiti in fabbrica e sospesi in situ.

Caramel desenvolveu um módulo padrão como elemento base de cada plataforma. Os módulos são simétricos na forma e podem ser combinados de forma aleatória que responda às necessidades de tamanho e forma pretendidos pelo cliente. Todos eles foram construídos na fábrica e suspensos in situ.

Caramel utvecklade en standardmodul som grundläggande beståndsdel för varje plattform. Modulerna är symmetriska i sin form och kan kombineras på ett slumpmässigt sätt som motsvarar kundens behov vad gäller storlek och form. Alla har byggts på fabrik och monterats på plats.

3-D view of the roof and the suspension points

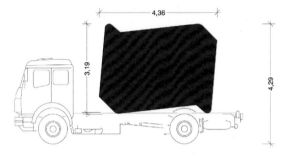

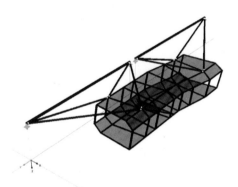

Structure in 3-D

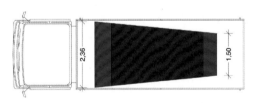

Illustration of transport of module using truck

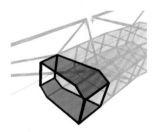

Standard module in 3-D

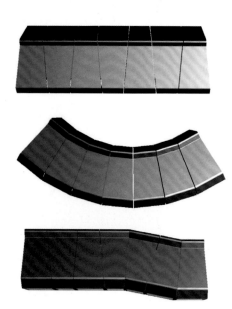

Concept of modular structure

Diagram of production modules

Standard module with furnishings in perspective

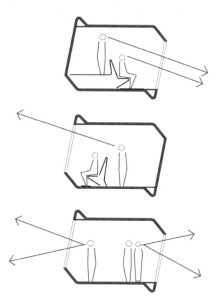

Section of possible views from the platform

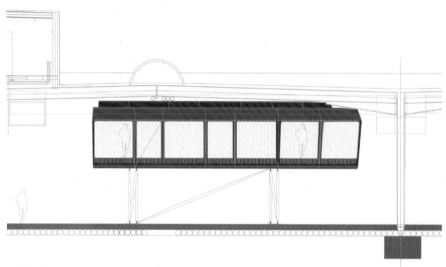

Longitudinal section

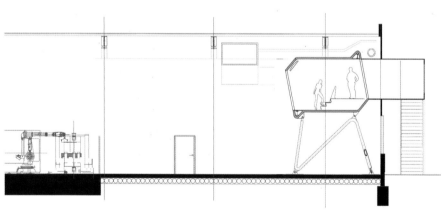

Transversal section

LOS CANTEROS SHELTER

Nicolás del Río, Max Núñez/dRN ARCHITECTS
Farellones, Chile
© Felipe Camus

The house is situated in a pre-existing space of a slope, bounded by two stone retaining walls that define the plane. A metal framework of pre-sized columns and beams were chosen to minimize the cost and construction time of the work.

Cette maison, en retrait sur une pente, est délimitée par deux murs de soutènement en pierre qui définissent le plan. Son ossature métallique, composée de piliers et de poutres sur mesure, minimise le coût et la durée de construction de l'habitation.

Das Haus befindet sich an einem vorher bestehenden Leerraum an einem Hang und ist von zwei Erdstützmauern abgegrenzt, welche die Ebene definieren. Man entschied sich für ein Metallstrukturskelett aus Pfosten und vorabgemessenen Trägern, welche Baukosten und –zeit minimieren.

Dit huis staat op een bestaand leeg stuk tegen een helling en wordt begrensd door twee stenen steunmuren die de plattegrond bepalen. Er is gekozen voor een metalen skelet van pilaren en balken; doordat deze vooraf op maat zijn gemaakt blijven de kosten en bouwtijd beperkt.

La casa se sitúa en el vacío preexistente de una pendiente, acotado por dos muros de contención de piedra que definen el plano. Se optó por un esqueleto de estructura metálica de pilares y vigas predimensionadas que minimizan el coste y tiempo de construcción de la obra.

La casa è situata alla base di un pendio preesistente, delimitato da due muri di sostegno in pietra che ne definiscono la pianta. È stato scelto uno scheletro metallico di pilastri e travi predimensionati per minimizzare i costi e i tempi di costruzione dell'opera.

A casa situa-se num espaço preexistente de uma ladeira, limitada por dois muros de contenção em pedra que definem o plano. Uma estrutura de metal de pilares e vigas pré-dimensionadas foram escolhidas para minimizar o custo e tempo de construção do trabalho.

Huset ligger på en sluttning, där det tidigare fanns ett tomrum, och det avgränsas av två stenmurar som definierar ritningen. En metallstomme med pelare och bjälkar valdes, vars storlekar är förbestämda vilket minimerar kostnaden och tiden som behövs för byggnadsarbetet.

North elevation

East elevation

West elevation

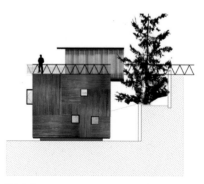

South elevation

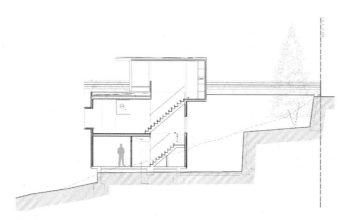

Section A-A

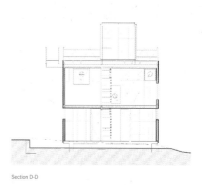

Section D-D

Ground floor

Second floor

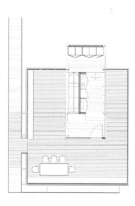

Terrace

MAGIC BOX

Jun Ueno, Magic Box, Inc.
Palos Verdes, CA, USA
© Magic Box, Inc.

Magic Box is a versatile box that changes the stereotypes of manufactured homes. Thanks to its cubic structure, it can be used as a separate space or within a larger one. It can be used as an office, studio or outdoor space. It also includes electrical conduits, ventilation systems (HVAC) or piping.

Magic Box est un cube polyvalent qui modifie les stéréotypes sur les habitations préfabriquées. Grâce à sa structure cubique, il peut être utilisé comme un espace séparé ou inclus dans un autre plus grand, et servir de bureau, studio ou espace extérieur. Il est également équipé d'une installation électrique, de systèmes de ventilation (HVAC) ou encore de canalisations.

Magic Box ist ein vielseitiger Kasten, der die Stereotypen der Fertighäuser umkrempelt. Dank seiner Würfelstruktur kann er als getrennter Raum oder innerhalb eines noch größeren Raums verwendet werden. Er kann als Büro, Studio oder Außenraum dienen. Er enthält außerdem Stromleitungen, Belüftungssysteme (HVAC) und Rohrleitungsinstallation.

De Magic Box is een veelzijdige box die het stereotype van de prefabwoning verandert. Dankzij de kubusvorm kan hij ingezet worden als afgescheiden ruimte of als ruimte binnen een grotere ruimte. Hij kan gebruikt worden als kantoor, studio of buitenruimte. Er kunnen ook elektricteitsleidingen, ventilatiesystemen (HVAC) of waterleidingen in verwerkt worden.

Magic Box es una caja versátil que cambia los estereotipos de las viviendas prefabricadas. Gracias a su estructura cúbica, puede ser usada como un espacio separado o dentro de uno más grande. Puede utilizarse como oficina, estudio o espacio exterior. Además, incluye conductos de electricidad, sistemas de ventilación (HVAC) o instalación de tuberías.

Magic Box è una scatola versatile che cambia gli stereotipi delle case prefabbricate. Grazie alla sua struttura cubica, può servire come spazio separato o all'interno di un ambiente più grande. Può diventare un ufficio, uno studio o uno spazio esterno. Inoltre comprende cablaggi elettrici, sistemi di ventilazione (HVAC) e tubazioni varie.

Magic Box é uma caixa versátil que altera os estereótipos das casas pré-fabricadas. Graças à sua estrutura cúbica, pode ser usada como um espaço separado ou dentro de um maior. Pode utilizar-se como escritório, estúdio ou espaço exterior. Inclui ainda, condutas de electricidade, sistemas de ventilação (HVAC) ou instalação de tubagens.

Magic Box är en flexibel låda som förändrar stereotyperna om monteringsfärdiga bostäder. Tack vare dess kubiska struktur kan den användas som ett separat utrymme eller inne i ett annat utrymme. Den kan användas som kontor, studio eller utvändig yta. Dessutom inkluderar den elledningar, ventilationssystem (HVAC) eller installation av rörsystem.

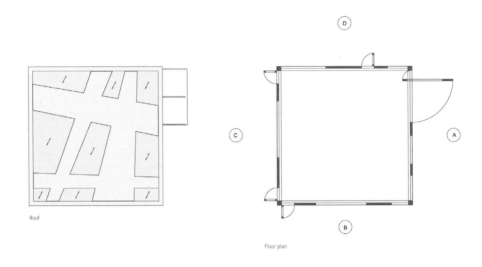

Roof

Floor plan

Section

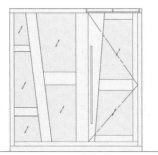

Elevation A

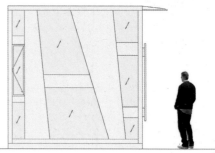

Elevation B

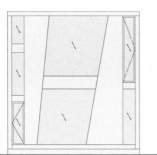

Elevation C

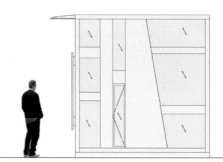

Elevation D

145

HOUSE **205**

David Lorente, Josep Ricart, Xavier Ros, Roger Tudó/H Arquitectes
Vacarisses, Spain
© Starp Estudi

To avoid damaging the land, the house is situated on a large platform of existing rock. A plywood structure with large format precast KLH panels for the walls and ceiling were used, anchored to the ground by two concrete struts. This structure reduces the CO_2 emissions associated with the foundation and structure.

Afin d'éviter d'endommager le terrain, la maison a été installée sur une grande plateforme de roche dans le sol. Les murs et le toit forment une structure de panneaux préfabriqués en bois stratifié de grand format KHL, qui repose sur le sol à l'aide de deux traverses en béton. Cette structure permet de réduire les émissions de CO_2 associées à la mise en place des fondations et de la structure.

Um Schäden am Gelände zu vermeiden, befindet sich das Gelände auf einer großen bestehenden Felsplattform. Für Wände und Decke wurde eine Struktur aus laminiertem Holz mit großformatigem Fertig-KLH verwendet, die auf dem Gelände mit Betonpfosten abgestützt ist. Mit dieser Struktur werden die dem Fundament und der Struktur zugeschriebenen CO_2 Abgaben reduziert.

Om schade aan het landschap te voorkomen is dit huis gebouwd op een groot bestaand rotsplateau. Er is gekozen voor een houten skelet met grote, geprefabriceerde KLH-panelen voor muren en plafonds. Het geheel steunt op het terrein door middel van twee betonnen schoren. Met deze constructie heeft men de CO_2-uitstoot waarmee het leggen van een fundering en de bouw gepaard gaan weten te omzeilen.

Para evitar dañar el terreno, la casa se sitúa sobre una gran plataforma de roca existente. Se utilizó una estructura de madera laminada con paneles de gran formato prefabricado KLH para muros y techo, apoyada al terreno mediante dos riostras de hormigón. Con esta estructura se reducen las emisiones de CO_2 asociadas a la cimentación y la estructura.

Per evitare di danneggiare il terreno, la casa poggia su una grande piattaforma di roccia esistente. È stata usata una struttura in legno multistrato con pannelli prefabbricati di grande formato KLH per pareti e soffitti, appoggiata a terra su due montanti in cemento. Questa struttura riduce le emissioni di CO_2 associate alle fondazioni e alla struttura portante.

Para evitar danificar o terreno, a casa assenta sobre numa grande plataforma de pedra já existente. Uma estrutura de madeira laminada com painéis KLH pré-fabricados de grande formato foi utilizada para as paredes e tecto, apoiados no chão por dois pilares de betão. Esta estrutura reduz as emissões de CO_2 associadas com a fundação e estrutura.

För att undvika skador på marken ligger huset på en stor plattform på en befintlig berggrund. Man använde en stomme av trälaminat med KLH-paneler i stort monteringsfärdigt format för väggar och tak, som stöds på marken av två tvärbalkar av betong. Med denna stomme minskar utsläppen av koldioxid som är förenade med grundläggning och stommen.

Longitudinal section

Transversal section

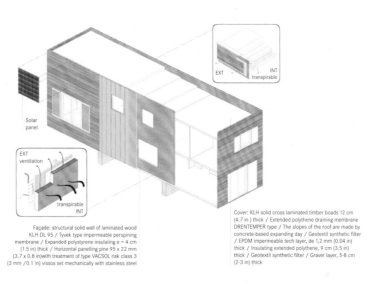

Solar panel

EXT   INT
    transpirable

EXT ventilation

transpirable INT

Façade: structural solid wall of laminated wood KLH DL 95 / Tyvek type impermeable perspining membrane / Expanded polystyrene insulating e = 4 cm (1.5 in) thick / Horizontal panelling pine 95 x 22 mm (3.7 x 0.8 in)with treatment of type VACSOL risk class 3 (3 mm /0.1 in) vissos set mechanically with stainless steel

Cover: KLH solid cross laminated timber boads 12 cm (4.7 in) thick / Extended polythene draining membrane DRENTEMPER type / The slopes of the roof are made by concrete-based expanding day / Geotextil synthetic filter / EPDM impermeable tech layer, de 1,2 mm (0.04 in) thick / Insulating extended polythene, 9 cm (3.5 in) thick / Geotextil synthetic filter / Graver layer, 5-8 cm (2-3 in) thick

Axonometric view

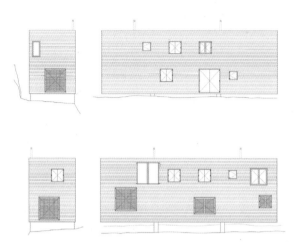

Elevations

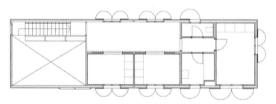

Second floor

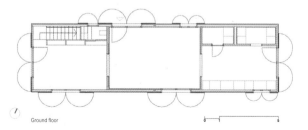

Ground floor

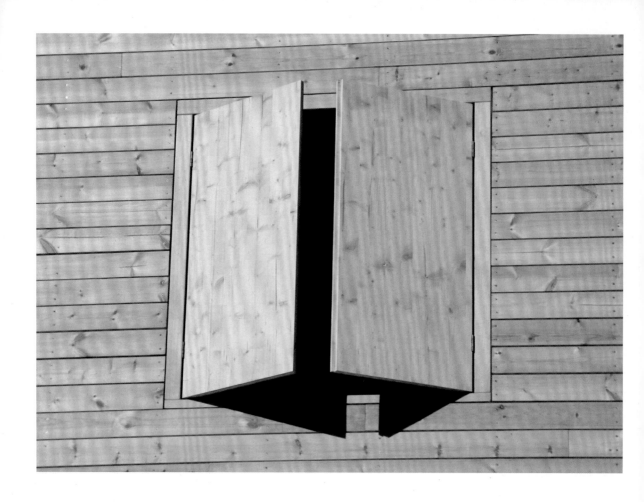

HOUSE IN **ESSEX ST**.

Andrew Maynard Architects
Brunswick, Australia
© Peter Bennetts, Dan Mahon

This project involves the extension of an already existing "weatherboard house". The new volume features a wooden frame fitted with recycled steel profiles of 12 mm (4.7 in) and is developed in the east-west axis. Its design responds to increased solar gain, which complements the light and thermal state of the home.

Ce projet consiste dans l'agrandissement d'une « weatherboard house » déjà construite. Le nouveau volume présente une structure en bois encastrée avec des profilés en acier recyclé de 12 mm et est orienté suivant l'axe est-ouest. Son design cherche à augmenter l'apport solaire, de manière à améliorer l'exposition lumineuse et la situation thermique de l'habitation principale.

Das Projekt umfasst die Erweiterung eines schon vorhandenen "weatherboard house". Das neue Volumen zeigt eine Holzstruktur, die anhand von 12 mm Trägern aus Recyclingstahl eingesetzt und in Ost-/Westachse ausgerichtet ist. Sein Entwurf entstand aus einer Erhöhung der Solarnutzung, mit der die Licht- und Wärmesituation der üblichen Wohnung ergänzt wird.

De project bestaat uit de uitbreiding van een bestaand weatherboard house. Het nieuwe stuk bestaat uit een houten structuur in profielen van gerecycled staal van 12 mm en bevindt zich aan de oost-westas. Het ontwerp is gericht op een verhoging van de opbrengst van zonne-energie, die de verlichting en verwarming van de bestaande woning aanvult.

Este proyecto consiste en la extensión de una *weatherboard house* ya existente. El nuevo volumen presenta una estructura de madera encajada mediante perfiles de acero reciclado de 12 mm y se desarrolla en el eje este-oeste. Su diseño responde a un aumento de la ganancia solar, que complemente la situación lumínica y térmica de la vivienda habitual.

Questo progetto prevede l'ampliamento di un'abitazione tipo "weatherboard house" già esistente. Il nuovo volume presenta una struttura in legno incassata mediante profili in acciaio riciclato di 12 mm e si sviluppa in direzione est-ovest. È stato progettato per aumentare il guadagno solare, integrando l'illuminazione e il riscaldamento dell'abitazione.

Este projecto consiste na extensão de uma "weatherboard house" já existente. O novo volume possui uma estrutura de madeira encaixada através de perfis de aço reciclado de 12 mm e é desenvolvida no eixo este-oeste. O seu desenho responde a um ganho solar mais elevado, que complementa a luminosidade e a situação térmica da casa.

Detta projekt består av utsträckning av ett redan befintligt "weatherboard house". Den nya volymen har en stomme av trä som är sammanfogad med profiler av återvunnet 12 mm-stål och den utvecklar sig i axeln öst-väst. Dess design motsvarar en ökad solvinst, som kompletterar den ordinarie bostadens ljus- och värmesituation.

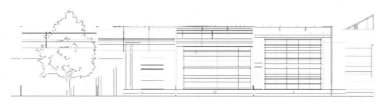

North elevation

South elevation

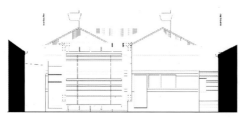

Construction details

East elevation

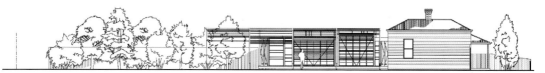

Longitudinal elevation with sections

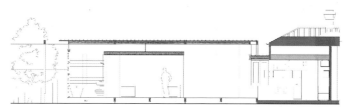

North longitudinal section

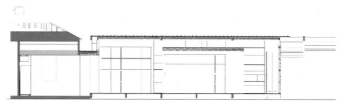

South longitudinal section

Views of the exterior in perspective

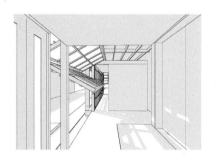
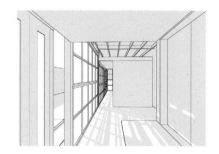
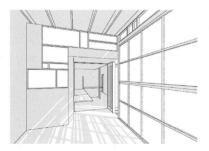
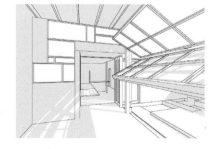

Views of the interior in perspective

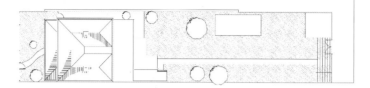

Plan of existing roof

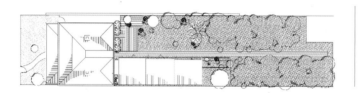

Plan of proposed roof

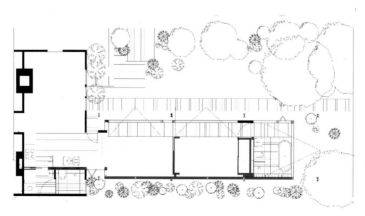

Proposed floor plan

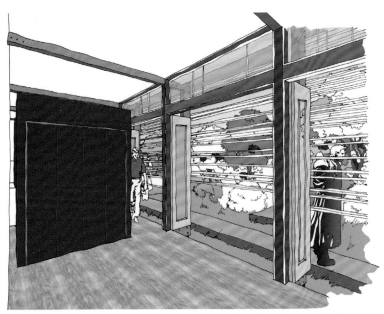

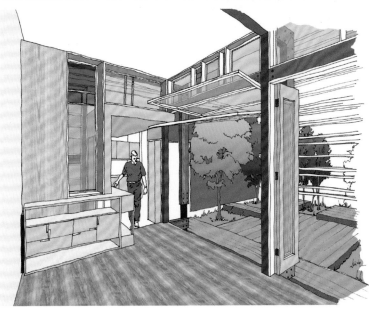

NOMADHOME

Hobby A. Schuster & Maul, Gerold Peham
Seekirchen am Wallersee, Austria
© Marc Haader

Nomadhome is a patented flexible construction consisting of the union of modules of 11 m^2 (118 sq ft). Its application can be commercial or residential. Modules can be interchangeable, expandable or disassembled at any time. The construction can be disassembled in 2-3 days and the modules can be transported by road.

Nomadhome est un système breveté de construction flexible qui consiste en l'assemblage de modules de 11 m^2. Son application peut être commerciale ou résidentielle. Les modules sont interchangeables entre eux, extensibles et peuvent être démontés à tout moment. La construction peut être démontée en 2 ou 3 jours et ses modules peuvent être transportés par la route.

Nomadhome ist ein patentiertes System flexibler Bauweise, das aus der Verbindung 11 m^2 großer Module besteht. Seine Anwendung kann kommerziell oder auch als Wohnung sein. Die Module können jederzeit untereinander ausgetauscht, erweitert o ausgebaut werden. Der Bau kann in 2-3 Tage demontiert und die Module können anschließend auf dem Landweg transportiert werden.

Nomadhome is een gepatenteerd flexibel bouwsysteem dat bestaat uit modulen van 11 m^2; het kan zowel commercieel als in de woningbouw toegepast worden. De modulen kunnen op elk moment onderling ingewisseld, uitgebreid of gedemonteerd worden. De hele constructie kan in 2-3 dagen uit elkaar gehaald worden en de modulen kunnen over de weg vervoerd worden.

Nomadhome es un sistema patentado de construcción flexible consistente en la unión de módulos de 11 m^2. Su aplicación puede ser comercial o residencial. Los módulos pueden ser intercambiables entre sí, expandibles o desensamblados en cualquier momento. La construcción puede ser desensamblada en 2-3 días y sus módulos, transportados por carretera.

Nomadhome è un sistema brevettato di costruzione flessibile che consiste nella giunzione di moduli di 11 m^2. La sua applicazione può essere sia commerciale che residenziale. I moduli sono intercambiabili, espandibili o smontabili in qualsiasi momento. La struttura può essere smontata nel giro di 2-3 giorni e i suoi moduli possono essere trasportati su strada.

Nomadhome é uma construção flexível patenteada que consiste na união de módulos de 11 m^2. A sua aplicação pode ser comercial ou residencial. Os módulos podem ser permutáveis, expansíveis ou desmontados a qualquer momento. A construção pode ser desmontada em 2-3 dias e os módulos podem ser transportados por estrada.

Nomadhome är ett patenterat system för flexibel konstruktion som består av sammanfogning av moduler som är 11 m^2. Den kan användas till kommersiella byggnader eller bostäder. Modulerna kan bytas ut sinsemellan, de kan expanderas eller monteras isär när som helst. Konstruktionen kan monteras isär på 2-3 dagar och modulerna kan transporteras på bilväg.

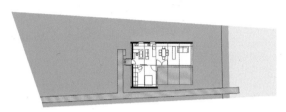

Site plan

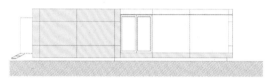

Southwest elevation

Northeast elevation

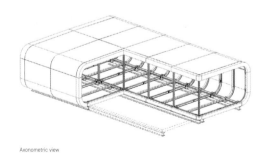

Axonometric view

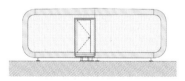

Southeast elevation

Northwest elevation

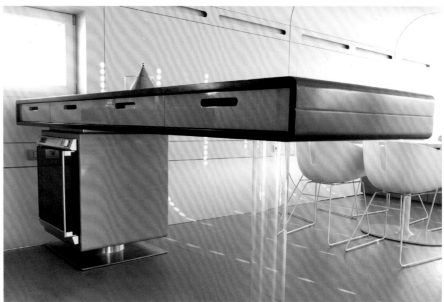

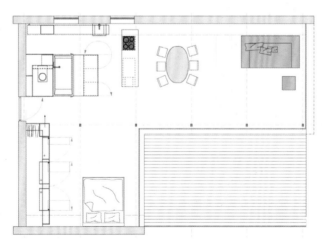

Floor plan of basic house

REF-RING

Atelier Tekuto
Zushi, Japan
© Makoto Yoshida

The arrangement of the panels at odd angles creates three-dimensional spaces, as if the house was twisted. Its structure is based on two twisted rings made from wood paneling, whose combination creates three-dimensional spaces. The creation of these directional axis causes an illusion of amplitude of space.

Les panneaux sont disposés en formant des angles étranges, qui permettent de créer des espaces tridimensionnels comme si la maison était déformée. Sa structure est basée sur deux cercles tordus, fabriqués avec des panneaux en bois, dont la combinaison crée des espaces tridimensionnels, suivant des axes directionnels qui donnent une sensation d'ampleur à l'espace.

Die Anordnung der Paneele in eigenartigen Winkeln bildet dreidimensionale Bereiche, als ob das Haus verbogen wäre. Seine Struktur basiert auf zwei verbogenen Ringen, die aus Holzpaneelen erstellt sind und deren Kombination dreidimensionale Bereiche bildet. Die Bildung dieser ausgerichteten Achsen erweckt den Eindruck der Großräumigkeit.

De plaatsing van de panelen in vreemde hoeken creëert driedimensionale ruimten, alsof het huis vervormd is. Het skelet is gebaseerd op twee verdraaide ringen van houten panelen, waarvan de combinatie driedimensionale ruimten schept; deze richtinggevende spilwerking wekt de illusie van ruimtelijkheid.

La disposición de los paneles en ángulos extraños crea espacios tridimensionales, como si la casa estuviese retorcida. Su estructura se basa en dos aros retorcidos y realizados con paneles de madera, cuya combinación crea espacios tridimensionales; la creación de estos axis direccionales provoca una ilusión de amplitud del espacio.

La disposizione dei pannelli ad angoli irregolari crea curiosi spazi tridimensionali, come se la casa fosse attorcigliata. La struttura è basata su due anelli ritorti e realizzata con pannelli di legno, la cui combinazione crea spazi tridimensionali; la creazione di questi assi direzionali provoca un'illusione di ampiezza dello spazio.

A disposição dos painéis em ângulos estranhos cria espaços tridimensionais, como se a casa estivesse retorcida. A sua estrutura baseia-se em dois anéis retorcidos feitos de painéis de madeira, cuja combinação cria espaços tridimensionais, a criação destes eixos direccionais causa uma ilusão de amplitude de espaço.

Placeringen av paneler i egendomliga vinklar skapar tredimensionella utrymmen, som om huset vore snedvridet. Dess stomme är baserad på två vridna ringar och har gjorts av träpaneler. Kombinationen av dessa skapar tredimensionella utrymmen. Skapandet av dessa axis i olika riktningar ger upphov till en sinnesvilla som gör att utrymmet verkar större.

Elevations

Section

Elevations

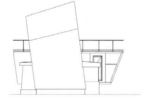

Section

Sections

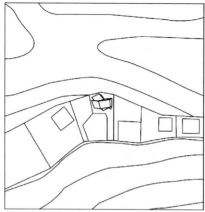

Site plan

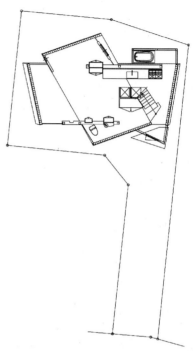

Ground floor

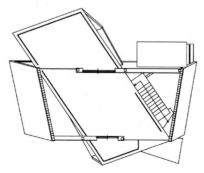

Second floor

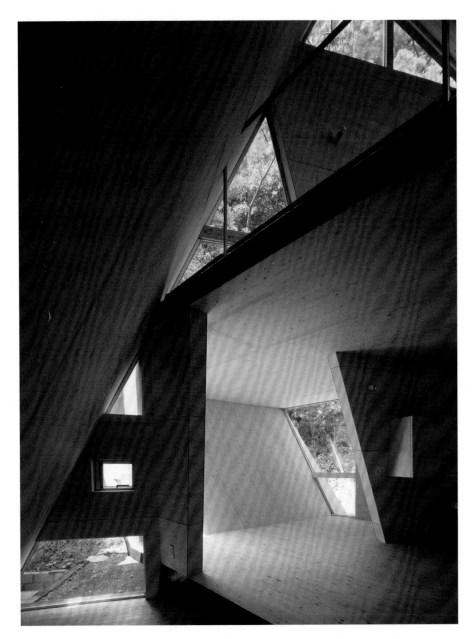

ZEROHOUSE

Occupation is advised throughout the year between latitudes 36° N and 36° S.
Between 47° N and 47° S, partial occupation is recommended.
© Devin Keyes, Frank Farkash, Scott Specht (renderings)

Although it is merely a prototype, zeroHouse is a representation of how a house can be sustainable in the present and future. It is formed by two rectangular volumes like a container. The electrical system is supported by a network of batteries that can work for a week without a ray of sunshine.

Même s'il ne s'agit encore que d'un prototype, zeroHouse symbolise à la perfection la maison durable d'aujourd'hui et de demain. Elle est constituée de deux volumes à base rectangulaire, de type container, et est équipée d'un système électrique alimenté par un bloc de batteries, dont l'autonomie peut aller jusqu'à une semaine sans soleil.

Obwohl es sich nur um einen Prototypen handelt, ist zeroHouse eine ausgezeichnete Repräsentation eines gegenwärtigen und zukünftigen nachhaltigen Hauses. Es besteht aus zwei Körpern mit rechteckigem Grundriss in der Art eines Containers. Die Stromversorgung wird durch ein Akkunetz mit einer Woche Autonomie ohne Sonne gelöst.

Hoewel het hier slechts om een prototype gaat, is zeroHouse een perfecte weergave van hoe het duurzame huis van het heden en de toekomst eruit kan zien. Het bestaat uit twee rechthoekige delen, containerstijl. Elektriciteit komt van een netwerk van accu's die een week zonder zon kunnen voor ze leeg zijn.

Aunque sólo se trate de un prototipo, zeroHouse es toda una representación de cómo puede ser la casa sostenible del presente y futuro. Está formada por dos cuerpos de planta rectangular a modo de contenedor. El sistema eléctrico se sustenta gracias a una red de baterías que tienen autonomía de una semana sin sol.

Anche se è solo un prototipo, zeroHouse è tutta una rappresentazione di come può essere la casa sostenibile del presente e del futuro. È formata da due corpi a pianta rettangolare, come un container. L'impianto elettrico è supportato da una rete di batterie che hanno un'autonomia di una settimana senza sole.

Apesar de ser meramente um protótipo, zeroHouse é uma representação de como uma casa pode ser sustentável no presente e futuro. É formada por dois volumes rectangulares como um contentor. O sistema eléctrico é suportado por uma rede de baterias que têm autonomia durante uma semana sem um único raio de sol.

Även om det bara handlar om en prototyp är zeroHouse en representation av hur nutidens och framtidens ekologiskt hållbara hus kan se ut. Det består av två kroppar med rektangulär planritning som en container. Det elektriska systemet upprätthålls tack vare ett nät av batterier som är oberoende av solen under en vecka.

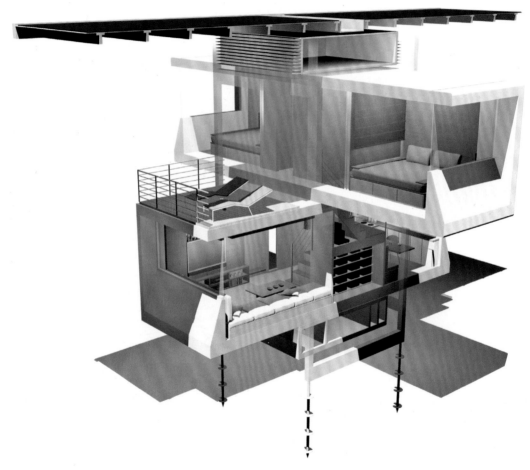

Perspective view

Bright white

Metallic silver

Deep marine

Forest green

Desert red

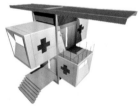

Custom graphics

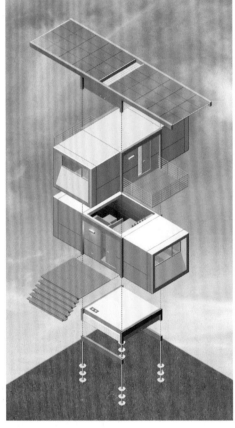

Exploded view

NEXT HOUSE **COLLECTION THÉA**

Magnus Ståhl
Stockholm, Sweden
© Christian Saltas

Next House is a developer of manufactured homes sold by catalog, which works with several Swedish builders and architects. It offers four different types of dwellings (XXS, S, M and L). This house for a childless couple is type L and measure 164 m² (1,765 sq ft). The construction took a total of seven and a half months.

Next House est un promoteur d'habitations préfabriquées en vente par catalogue, qui travaille avec différents constructeurs et architectes suédois. Il propose des habitations avec quatre typologies différentes (XXS, S, M et L). La maison présentée ici, de typologie L, a été construite pour un couple sans enfants et dispose de 164 m². Sa construction a duré sept mois et demi au total.

Next House ist ein Bauunternehmen, das Fertighäuser per Katalog verkauft und für verschiedene schwedische Baufirmen und Architekten arbeitet. Es bietet Häuser in vier verschiedenen Bauweisen (XXS, S, M und L) an. Dieses Haus für ein kinderloses Paar gehört zur Bauweise L und ist 164 m² groß. Der Bau dauerte insgesamt siebeneinhalb Monate.

Next House is een ontwikkelaar van prefabhuizen die per catalogus verkocht worden. Er wordt gewerkt met verschillende Zweedse bouwbedrijven een architecten. Next House biedt vier verschillende typen woningen aan (XXS, S, M en L). De woning voor een stel zonder kinderen behoort tot het type L en is 164 m² groot. De bouw duurde in totaal 7,5 maand.

Next House es una promotora de viviendas prefabricadas de venta por catálogo que trabaja con diferentes constructores y arquitectos suecos. Ofrece viviendas de cuatro tipologías diferentes (XXS, S, M y L). Esta vivienda para una pareja sin hijos pertenece a la tipología L y dispone de 164 m². La construcción duró un total de siete meses y medio.

Next House promuove abitazioni prefabbricate in vendita su catalogo, lavorando con diversi costruttori e architetti svedesi. Offre abitazioni di quattro tipi diversi (XXS, S, M e L). Questa abitazione per una coppia senza figli appartiene al tipo L e occupa una superficie di 164 m². La costruzione è durata in tutto sette mesi e mezzo.

Next House é uma promotora de casas pré-fabricadas vendidas por catálogo, que trabalha com vários construtores e arquitectos suecos. Oferece quatro tipos diferentes de habitações (XXS, S, M e L). Esta casa para um casal sem filhos é do tipo L e mede 164 m². A construção durou um total de sete meses e meio.

NextHouse är en byggherre som tillverkar monteringsfärdiga bostäder som säljs via katalog, och som jobbar med olika svenska byggbolag och arkitekter. Next House erbjuder fyra olika typer av bostäder (XXS, S, M och L). Denna bostad för ett par utan barn tillhör typen L och är 164 m². Byggnadsarbetet tog totalt sju och en halv månad.

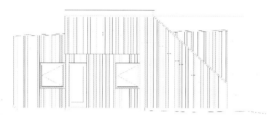

Northwest elevation

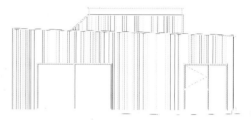

Southeast elevation

Southwest elevation

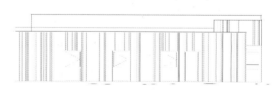

Northeast elevation

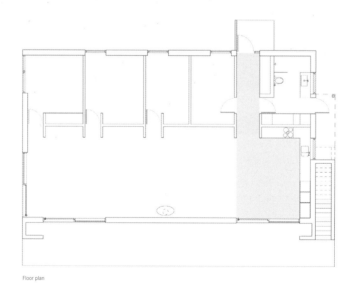

Floor plan

X HOUSE

Arquitectura X
Quito, Ecuador
© Sebastián Crespo

This house is sitting on a plot of 380 m²(4,094 sq ft). The building consists of a lightweight structure on a concrete pedestal, around which an oxidized steel rectangular box and coated plywood is mounted on the interior. The service and circulation spaces are arranged around a closed white polycarbonate volume.

Cette habitation est construite sur un terrain de 380 m². Le bâtiment est composé d'une structure légère, qui repose sur une base en béton et sur laquelle est montée une enveloppe rectangulaire revêtue d'acier oxydé et de contreplaqué à l'intérieur. Les espaces de service et les passages sont disposés dans un volume blanc fermé en polycarbonate.

Dieses Haus steht auf einem 380 m² großen Grundstück. Das Gebäude besteht aus einer leichten Struktur auf Betonsockel, auf dem der rechteckige, oxidierte und innen furnierte Stahlkasten aufgebaut wird. Die Dienstleistungs- und Verkehrsbereiche liegen um ein weißes, geschlossenes Polykarbonatvolumen herum.

Deze woning staat op een perceel van 380 m². Ze heeft een licht skelet op een betonnen basis, met daaromheen een rechthoekige box bekleed met geöxideerd gelaagd staal aan de binnenkant. De gebruiks- en verbindingsruimten zijn verdeeld over een gesloten wit geheel van polycarbonaat.

Esta vivienda está asentada en un solar de 380 m². El edificio está compuesto por una estructura ligera sobre un pedestal de hormigón, entorno a la cual se monta una caja rectangular revestida de acero oxidado y contrachapado en el interior. Los espacios de servicio y circulación están dispuestos dentro de un volumen blanco cerrado de policarbonato.

Questa abitazione sorge in un terreno di 380 m². L'edificio è costituito da una struttura leggera su un piedistallo di cemento, attorno al quale è montata una scatola rettangolare rivestita in acciaio ossidato e compensato all'interno. Gli spazi di servizio e di transito sono disposti all'interno di un volume chiuso bianco in policarbonato.

Esta casa assenta numa área de 380 m². O edifício é composto por uma estrutura leve sobre um pedestal de betão, em redor do qual se monta uma caixa rectangular revestida de aço oxidado e contraplacado no interior. Os espaços de serviço e circulação estão dispostos dentro de um volume branco fechado de policarbonato.

Denna bostad ligger på en tomt som är 380 m². Byggnaden består av en lätt stomme över ett betongfundament, runt vilken en rektangulär kub monteras, som är klädd av oxiderat stål och har plywood invändigt. Förrådsutrymmena och hallen finns i en vit stängd volym av polykarbonatfiberfiber.

Deconstructed axonometric view

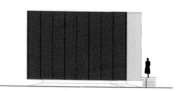

North elevation

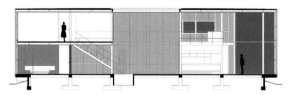

West elevation

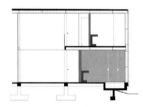

Longitudinal section

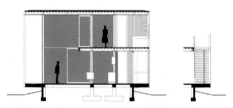

Transversal section 1

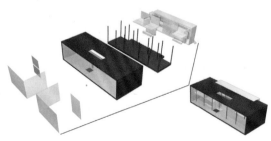

Transversal section 2

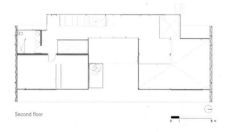

Second floor

0 I   5 M

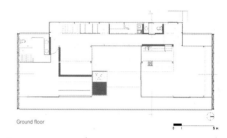

Ground floor

0 I   5 M

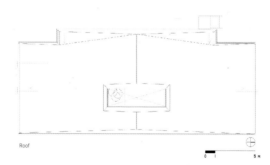

Roof

0 I   5 M

MODULAR **4**

Studio 804
Kansas City, KS, USA
© Studio 804

This house consists of a volume of one floor plus basement. A total of 139 m² (1,496 sq ft). The use of modular furniture facilitates the flexible organization of space. The house includes a large amount of recycled and eco-efficient components in its composition. It took three months to construct this model.

Cette habitation de 139 m² dispose d'un volume à un seul niveau, ainsi que d'un sous-sol. Elle est équipée d'un mobilier modulaire, qui facilite une organisation flexible de l'espace, et est composée d'un grand nombre d'éléments recyclés et énergétiquement efficaces. La construction de ce modèle a duré trois mois.

Dieses Haus besteht aus einem Volumen mit nur einer Etage und Untergeschoss. Insgesamt ist es 139 m² groß. Der Einsatz von Modulmöbeln erleichtert die flexible Raumgestaltung. Das Haus enthält eine Vielzahl recycelter und ökoeffizienter Bauteile in seinem Aufbau und die Bauzeit dieses Modells betrug drei Monate.

Deze woning bestaat uit één verdieping plus kelder. De totale oppervlakte bedraagt 139 m². Door het gebruik van modulair meubilair kan de ruimte flexibel ingericht worden. Bij de constructie van de woning is gebruikgemaakt van veel gerecyclede en ecologisch verantwoorde componenten. De bouw van dit model duurde drie maanden.

Esta vivienda consta de un volumen de una sola planta más sótano. En total dispone de 139 m². El uso de mobiliario modular facilita la organización flexible del espacio. La vivienda incluye una gran cantidad de componentes reciclados y ecoeficientes en su composición. La construcción de este modelo duró tres meses.

Questa abitazione è formata da un volume di un solo piano, più il seminterrato. Offre una superficie totale di 139 m². L'uso di mobili componibili facilita l'organizzazione flessibile dello spazio. La casa comprende una grande quantità di componenti riciclati ed ecoefficienti nella loro composizione. La costruzione di questo modello è durata tre mesi.

Esta casa consta de um volume de um só piso mais cave. No total dispõe de 139 m². A utilização de mobiliário modular facilita a organização flexível do espaço. A casa inclui uma grande quantidade de componentes reciclados e ecoeficientes na sua composição. A construção deste modelo durou três meses.

Denna bostad består av en volym med en våning samt en källare. Totalt är den 139 m². Användning av modulmöbler underlättar en flexibel organisering av utrymme. Bostaden har ett stort antal beståndsdelar som är återvunna och som är miljöeffektiva i sin sammansättning. Byggnationen av denna modell tog tre månader.

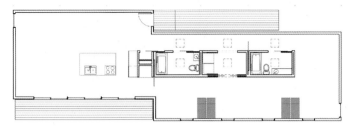

Floor plan A

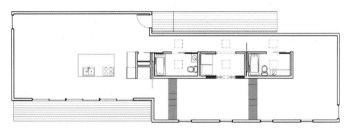

Floor plan B

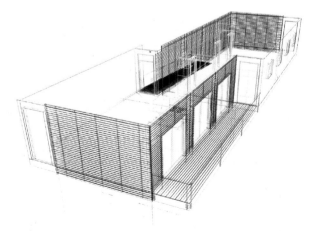

Perspective diagram

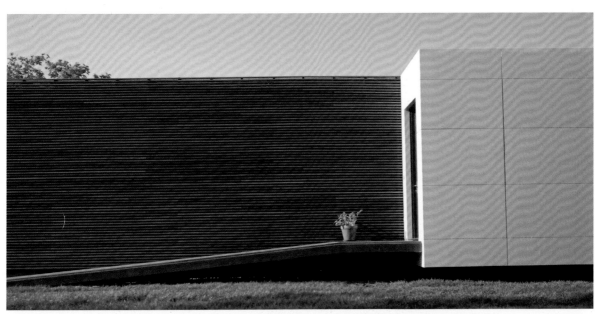

BLACK BOX

Matthias R. Schmalohr
Krainhagen, Germany
© Klaus Dieter Weiss

This property of 210 m² (2,260 sq ft) with two floors and basement is situated on a plot of 672 m² (7,233 sq ft). The construction of prefabricated elements was carried out in three weeks, two at the factory and one on site. The box is a dry system and total cost was lower than that of a standard house constructed in a conventional manner.

Cette habitation de 210 m² à deux étages et un sous-sol est située sur une parcelle de 672 m². Le montage des éléments fabriqués a été réalisé en trois semaines, deux en usine et une sur place. L'ensemble a été monté à sec et son coût total est inférieur à celui d'une maison standard construite de manière conventionnelle.

Dieses 210 m² große, zweistöckige Haus mit Untergeschoss steht auf einem 672 m² großen Grundstück. Der Bau der Fertigbauteile erfolgte in drei Wochen, zwei Wochen in der Fabrik und eine Woche vor Ort. Der Kasten wurde trocken montiert und die Gesamtkosten waren niedriger als die eines auf herkömmliche Art gebauten Standardhauses.

Deze woning van 210 m² met twee verdiepingen en een kelder staat op een perceel van 672 m². De prefabelementen werden in drie weken in elkaar gezet, twee in de fabriek en een ter plekke. De doos zonder mortel gebouwd. En de totale kosten waren lager dan die van een op conventionele wijze gebouwde standaardwoning.

Esta vivienda de 210 m² con dos plantas y sótano está situada en una parcela de 672 m². La construcción de elementos prefabricados se realizó en tres semanas, dos en fábrica y una en el emplazamiento. La caja se montó en seco y el coste total fue menor que el de una casa estándar construida de manera convencional.

Questa abitazione di 210 m² con due piani e seminterrato si trova in un terreno di 672 m². La costruzioni degli elementi prefabbricati si è conclusa in tre settimane, due in fabbrica e una in cantiere. La scatola è stata montata a secco e il costo totale è stato inferiore a quello di una casa standard costruita in modo convenzionale.

Esta casa de 210 m² com dois pisos e cave está situada numa parcela de 672 m². A construção de elementos pré-fabricados realizou-se em três semanas, duas em fábrica e uma no local. A caixa montou-se a seco e o custo total foi menor que o de uma casa padrão construída de forma convencional.

Denna bostad på 210 m² med två våningar och källare ligger på en tomt som är 672 m². Byggnationen av monteringsfärdiga beståndsdelar tog tre veckor, varav två veckor på fabriken och en vecka för placering. Kuben monterades med en gång och totalkostnaden var mindre än kostnaden för ett standardhus som byggs på konventionellt sätt.

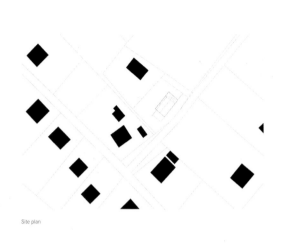

Site plan

Southeast elevation

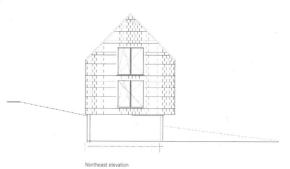

Northeast elevation

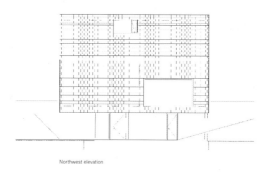

Northwest elevation

Southwest elevation

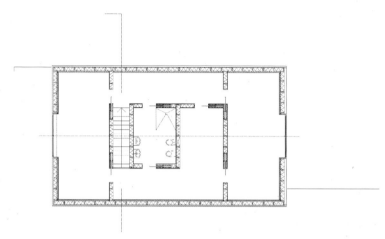

Second floor

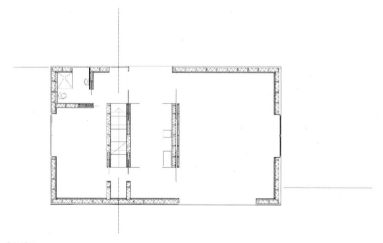

Ground floor

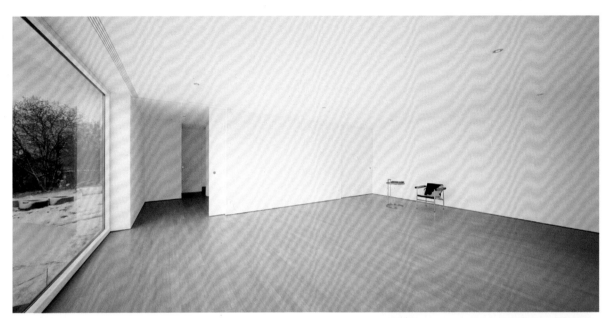

HOUSE OF **HUTS**

Studio NL-D
Breda, The Netherlands
© Hans Werlemann/Hectic Pictures

The project is organized in a main body designed as a residence and small auxiliary volumes in the garden: two cabins used as an office, a greenhouse and a sauna. Both the main building and the annexes are prefabricated.

Le projet consiste en un corps principal destiné à la résidence principale et en petits espaces auxiliaires dans le jardin : deux cabanes utilisées comme bureau, une serre et un sauna. Aussi bien le bâtiment principal que les annexes sont des éléments préfabriqués.

Das Projekt gliedert sich in einen Hauptkörper als Wohnhaus und einige kleine Nebenvolumina im Garten auf: Zwei Hütten, die als Büro genutzt werden, ein Wintergarten und eine Sauna. Das Hauptgebäude, wie auch die Nebengebäude, sind Fertigbauteile.

Dit project is opgebouwd uit een hoofddeel dat als woning dienst zou moeten doen en enkele kleine bijgebouwtjes in de tuin: twee hutten gebruikt als kantoor, een kas en een sauna. Zowel het hoofdgebouw als de bijgebouwtjes zijn geprefabriceerd.

El proyecto está organizado en un cuerpo principal pensado como residencia y unos pequeños volúmenes auxiliares en el jardín: dos cabañas usadas como oficina, un invernadero y una sauna. Tanto el edificio principal como los anexos son elementos prefabricados.

Il progetto si articola in un corpo principale destinato a residenza e in piccoli volumi ausiliari nel giardino: due cabine utilizzate come ufficio, una serra e una sauna. Sia l'edificio principale che gli altri elementi sono prefabbricati.

O projecto está organizado num corpo principal pensado como residência e pequenos volumes auxiliares no jardim: duas cabanas usadas como oficina, uma estufa e uma sauna. Tanto o edifício principal como os anexos são elementos pré-fabricados.

Projektet är organiserat med en huvudbyggnad som är tänkt som bostad och några mindre byggnader i trädgården. Två stugor används som kontor, växthus och bastu. Både huvudbyggnaden och annexen är monteringsfärdiga beståndsdelar.

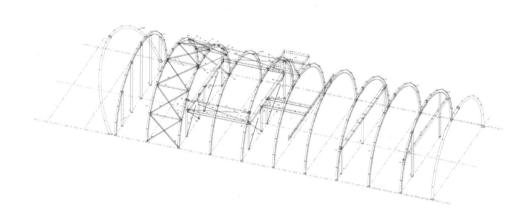

Diagram of the scaffold

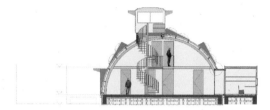

Sections

Ground floor

Second floor

THE FLOATING HOUSE

Ronan and Erwan Bouroullec
Chatou, France
© Paul Tahon, Ronan and Erwan Bouroullec

The houseboat has a rectangular plan measuring 5 x 23 m (16 x 75 ft) and a total area of 115 m² (1,237 sq ft), 23 m² (247 sq ft) of which are occupied by the two terraces. The main constructive volume is a wooden frame covered by an aluminium roof. The spaces, designed to live and work, are open and natural looking.

La maison flottante possède une base rectangulaire de 5 x 23 m et une surface totale de 115 m², dont 23 m² sont occupés par les deux terrasses. Le principal élément du volume de construction est une ossature en bois revêtue d'une toiture en aluminium. Les espaces, conçus à la fois pour vivre et travailler, sont ouverts et présentent un aspect naturel.

Das Hausboot besitzt einen rechteckigen, 5 x 23 m großen Grundriss, d. h. insgesamt 115 m² Fläche, von denen 23 m² von beiden Terrassen belegt sind. Das Hauptelement des Bauvolumens ist ein mit einer Aluminiumabdeckung verkleidetes Holzskelett. Die zum Leben und Arbeiten vorgesehenen Räume sind offen mit natürlicher Optik.

Dit drijvende huis heeft een rechthoekige woonlaag van 5 x 23 m en een totaal oppervlak van 115 m², waarvan 23 m² in beslag wordt genomen door de twee terrassen. Het hoofdelement van de bouwconstructie is een met aluminium afgedekt houten skelet. De ruimten voor wonen en werken zijn open en zien er natuurlijk uit.

La casa flotante tiene una planta rectangular de 5 x 23 m y una superficie total de 115 m², 23 m² de los cuales están ocupados por las dos terrazas. El elemento principal del volumen constructivo es un esqueleto de madera revestido por una cubierta de aluminio. Los espacios, pensados para vivir y trabajar, son abiertos y de aspecto natural.

La casa galleggiante ha una pianta rettangolare di 5 x 23 m e una superficie totale di 115 m², 23 m² dei quali occupati dalle due terrazze. L'elemento principale del volume costruttivo è una struttura portante in legno con una copertura in alluminio. Lo spazio, progettato per vivere e lavorare, ha un aspetto aperto e naturale.

A casa flutuante tem uma planta rectangular de 5 x 23 m m e uma superfície total de 115 m², 23 m² dos quais estão ocupados pelos dois terraços. O elemento principal do volume construtivo é uma armação de madeira revestida por uma cobertura de alumínio. Os espaços, pensados para viver e trabalhar, são abertos e de aspecto natural.

Det flytande huset har en rektangulär planlösning på 5 x 23 m m och en total yta på 115 m², 23 m², som upptas av två terrasser. Den viktigaste beståndsdelen i byggnadsvolymen är en trästomme med aluminiumbeklädnad. Utrymmena är tänkta för att leva och arbeta, de är öppna och har ett naturligt utseende.

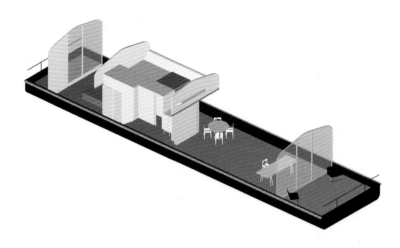

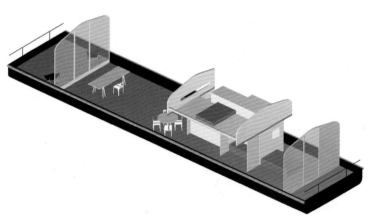

Axonometric view of the interior compartmentalization

LOBLOLLY HOUSE

KieranTimberlake Associates
Taylors Islands, MD, USA
© Barry Halkin

The volume consists of prefabricated elements that were assembled in situ in just six weeks. The main elements are the aluminum structure, fibercement siding, wooden paneling, polycarbonate-type hangar doors with an aluminum trim and birch plywood interiors.

Cette construction est composée d'éléments préfabriqués, qui ont été assemblés sur place en seulement six semaines. Elle est principalement constituée d'une structure en aluminium, de panneaux en fibrociment, d'un revêtement en bois, de portes de type hangar en polycarbonate avec un cadre en aluminium et de finitions intérieures en contreplaqué de bouleau.

Das Bauvolumen besteht komplett aus Fertigbauteilen, die in nur sechs Wochen vor Ort zusammengebaut wurden. Die wichtigsten Bauteile dabei sind die Aluminiumstruktur, Faserzementpaneele, Holzverkleidung, hangarartige Polykarbonattüren mit Aluminiumprofil und Innenausführungen aus Birkenfurnier.

Dit bouwwerk bestaat uit prefabelementen die ter plekke in slechts zes weken in elkaar gezet werden. De belangrijkste elementen zijn het skelet van aluminium, de panelen van vezelcement, de houten bekleding, de hangardeuren van polycarbonaat met aluminium posten en de berkenhouten afwerking van het interieur.

El volumen constructivo está formado por elementos prefabricados, que fueron ensamblados in situ en sólo seis semanas. Los elementos principales son la estructura de aluminio, los paneles de fibrocemento, el revestimiento de madera, las puertas tipo hangar de policarbonato con perfil de aluminio y los acabados interiores de contrachapado de abedul.

Il volume costruttivo è composto da elementi prefabbricati che sono stati assemblati in situ in sole sei settimane. Gli elementi principali sono la struttura in alluminio, i pannelli in fibrocemento, il rivestimento in legno, le porte tipo hangar di policarbonato con profilo di alluminio e le rifiniture interne in compensato di betulla.

O volume construtivo é formado por elementos pré-fabricados, que foram ensamblados *in situ* em apenas seis semanas. Os elementos principais são a estrutura de alumínio, os painéis de fibrocimento, o revestimento de madeira, as portas tipo hangar de policarbonato com perfil de alumínio e os acabamentos interiores de contraplacado de bétula.

Byggnadsvolymen består av monteringsfärdiga beståndsdelar som har sammanfogats på plats, vilket endast tog sex veckor. De viktigaste delarna är stommen av aluminium, panelerna av fibercement och beklädnaden av trä, dörrarna av hangartyp som är gjorda av polykarbonatfiberfiber med aluminiumprofil och den invändiga finishen av plywood från björk.

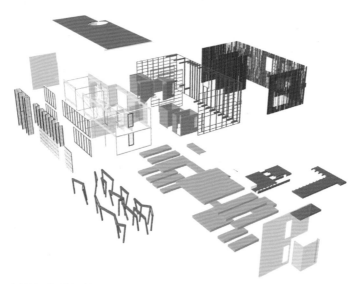

Exploded view with prefabricated elements

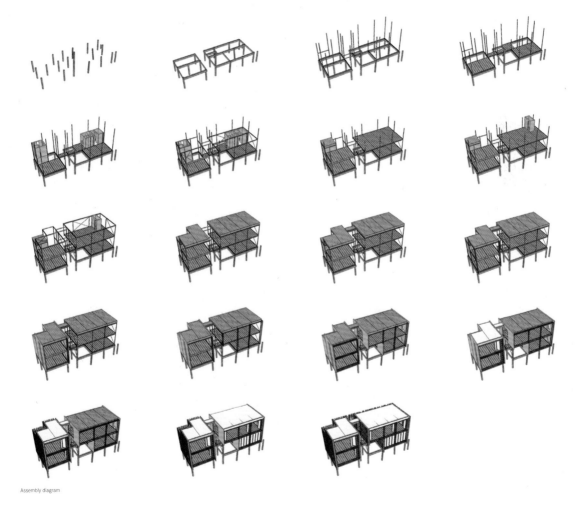

Assembly diagram

West elevation

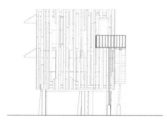

South elevation

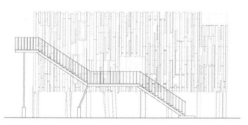

East elevation

North elevation

PALMS HOUSE

Marmol Radziner Prefab
Venice, CA, USA
© David Lena

The housing incorporates different environmental aspects as a recyclable steel structure and
SIP structural panels that reduce heating needs by 12-14%. As well as triple-glazed glass, natural
materials, low VOC paints and cross ventilation. Besides, its pefabricated construction process
significantly reduces the environmental impacts of construction.

L'habitation comporte divers éléments écologiques, comme la structure en acier recyclable
et les panneaux structurels SIP, qui réduisent les besoins thermiques de 12 à 14 %.
Du triple vitrage, des matériaux naturels, des peintures à faible teneur en COV et des systèmes
de ventilation transversale sont également utilisés. De plus, son procédé de construction
préfabriqué réduit considérablement l'impact environnemental.

Das Haus beinhaltet verschiedene Umweltschutzaspekte, wie eine Struktur aus recyceltem
Stahl und SIP Strukturpaneele, welche den Wärmebedarf um 12 – 14 % senken. Dazu gehören
auch dreifach verglaste Fenster, natürliche Baustoffe, Farben mit niedrigem COV-Gehalt und
Querbelüftungssysteme. Dazu kommt, dass seine Fertigbauweise die Umweltauswirkungen des
Baus deutlich reduziert.

Deze woning bevat diverse milieuvriendelijke oplossingen, zoals een skelet van gerecycled staal
en structureel geïsoleerde panelen (SIP), die de energie benodigd voor de verwarming met 12-
14% verlagen. Verder zijn er ramen met driedubbel glas, natuurlijke materialen, verven met een
laag gehalte vluchtige organische stoffen (VOS) en kruisventilatiesystemen. Tot slot zorgt het
prefabbouwproces voor een aanzienlijk kleinere milieu-aanslag op de omgeving.

La vivienda incorpora diversos aspectos ambientales como una estructura de acero reciclable y
paneles estructurales SIP que reducen las necesidades térmicas un 12-14%, y también cristales
de triple vidrio, materiales naturales, pinturas bajas en COV y sistemas de ventilación cruzada.
Aparte, este proceso de construcción reduce considerablemente los impactos ambientales.

L'abitazione presenta diversi aspetti ecologici come una struttura in acciaio riciclabile e
pannelli strutturali SIP che riducono il fabbisogno di riscaldamento del 12-14%. Sono presenti
anche finestre con tripli vetri, materiali naturali, vernici a basso contenuto di COV e sistemi
di ventilazione incrociata. Inoltre, il processo di costruzione prefabbricato riduce in modo
significativo l'impatto ambientale della costruzione.

A casa incorpora diversos aspectos ambientais como uma estrutura de aço reciclável e painéis
estruturais SIP que reduzem as necessidades térmicas em 12-14%. Tem também vidros triplos,
materiais naturais, pinturas baixas em COV e sistemas de ventilação cruzada. O seu processo de
construção pré-fabricado reduz consideravelmente os impactos ambientais da construção.

Bostaden har diverse miljömässiga aspekter såsom en återvunnen stomme i stål och strukturella
SIP-paneler som minskar behovet av uppvärmning 12-14%. Dessutom har bostaden fönster med
trippelglas, naturmaterial, målarfärg med låga halter av flyktiga organiska föreningar samt system
för korsventilation. Dessutom minskas miljöpåverkan på ett märkbart sätt i och med dess
monteringsfärdiga byggnadssätt.

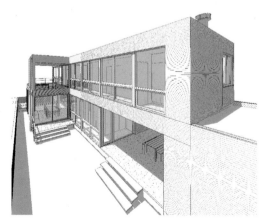

Rendering

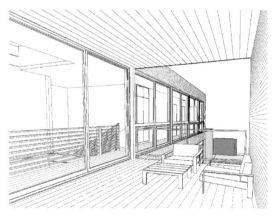

Computer illustration

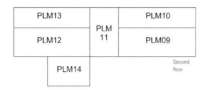

PLM13	PLM 11	PLM10
PLM12		PLM09
PLM14		

Second floor

Second floor

PLM08	PLM 05	PLM04	PLM 02	PLM 01
PLM07		PLM03		
PLM06				

Ground floor

Module layout by floor

Lower level / upper level

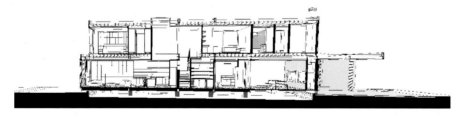

Section

SOLAR ACTIVE HOUSE

Architekturbüro Reinberg
Überfeld, Austria
© Fa. Sonnenkraft Österreich, Horst Danner

This home-show house designed for an Austrian prefabricated house company, meets requirements similar to the standard *Passiv Haus*, such as very good insulation in façades and bioclimatic design to facilitate solar gain. The house is self-sufficient in terms of energy, so that you get a zero balance because it produces all the energy it consumes.

Cette maison-prototype, conçue par un constructeur autrichien d'habitations préfabriquées, remplit des exigences semblables à celles du modèle *Passiv Haus*, telles qu'une bonne isolation au niveau des façades et une conception bioclimatique qui favorise l'apport solaire. L'habitation est énergétiquement autosuffisante, c'est-à-dire que son bilan est nul puisqu'elle produit toute l'énergie qu'elle consomme.

Dieses Vorzeigehaus, das für eine österreichische Fertighausfirma entworfen wurde, erfüllt mit einer guten Fassadenisolierung und bioklimatischem Design zur Verbesserung der Solarnutzung ähnliche Anforderungen wie der *Passivhaus* Standard. Das Haus ist energiemäßig selbstständig und gleicht seine Bilanz aus, indem es seinen gesamten Energieverbrauch auch erzeugt.

Dit showmodel, dat werd ontworpen voor een Oostenrijks bedrijf voor prefabwoningen, vodoet aan vergelijkbare eisen als het standaard *Passiv Haus*, zoals een zeer goede gevelisolatie en een bioklimatologisch ontwerp met zonnepanelen. Het huis is wat betreft energieverbruik zelfvoorzienend en komt uit op een nulbalans, want alle energie die nodig is, wordt zelf geproduceerd.

Esta vivienda-demostrador, diseñada para una compañía de vivienda prefabricada austríaca, cumple unos requisitos similares al estándar *Passiv Haus*, como son un muy buen aislamiento en fachadas y un diseño bioclimático que facilita la ganancia solar. La vivienda es energéticamente autosuficiente, de manera que se consigue un balance cero ya que produce toda la energía que consume.

Questa dimostrazione di abitazione, progettata per un'azienda austriaca di prefabbricati, soddisfa requisiti simili allo standard *Passiv Haus*, per esempio un ottimo isolamento delle pareti e un design bioclimatico per facilitare il guadagno solare. La casa è energeticamente autosufficiente, in modo da ottenere un bilancio energetico pari a zero, poiché produce tutta l'energia che consuma.

Esta casa-modelo, desenhada para uma empresa de casas pré-fabricadas austríaca, cumpre certos requisitos similares ao padrão *Passiv Haus*, tais como, um muito bom isolamento em fachadas e um desenho bioclimático que facilita o ganho solar. A casa é energeticamente auto-suficiente, de maneira que se consegue um balanço zero já que produz toda a energia que consume.

Denna visningsbostad är designad för en österrikisk kampanj om monteringsfärdiga bostäder. Den uppfyller liknande krav som standardmodellen *Passiv Haus*, såsom god isolering i fasaderna och bioklimatisk design som möjliggör tillvaratagandet av solenergin. Bostaden är energimässigt självförsörjande. Balansen är noll, eftersom bostaden förbrukar all energi som den producerar.

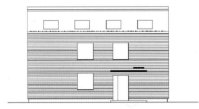

North elevation

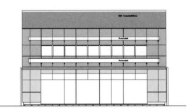

South elevation

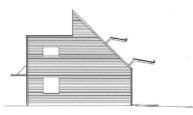

West elevation

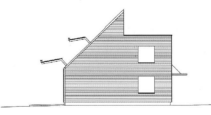

East elevation

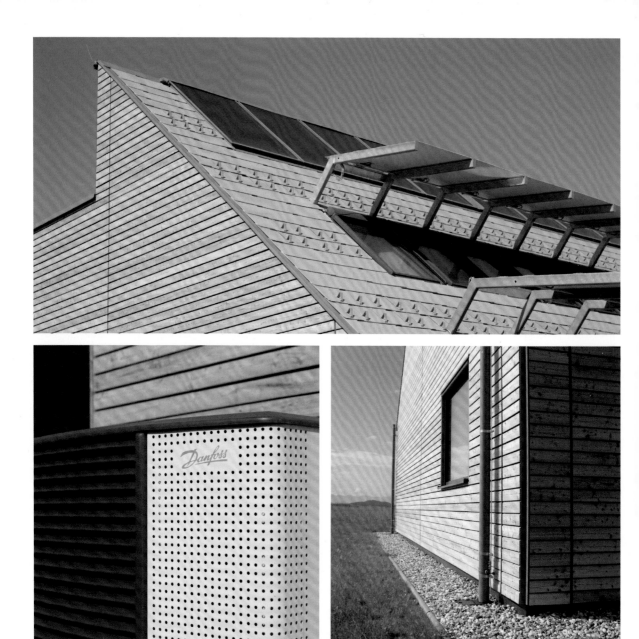

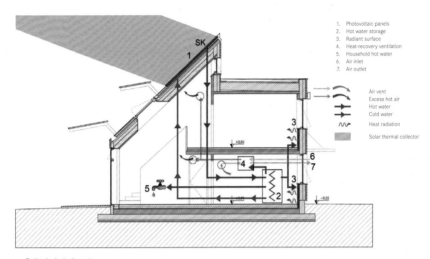

1. Photovoltaic panels
2. Hot water storage
3. Radiant surface
4. Heat-recovery ventilation
5. Household hot water
6. Air inlet
7. Air outlet

Air vent
Excess hot air
Hot water
Cold water
Heat radiation
Solar thermal collector

Section showing heating system

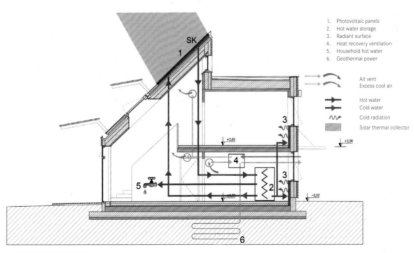

1. Photovoltaic panels
2. Hot water storage
3. Radiant surface
4. Heat recovery ventilation
5. Household hot water
6. Geothermal power

Ait vent
Excess cool air
Hot water
Cold water
Cold radiation
Solar thermal collector

Section showing cooling system

PLUS HOUSE

Claesson Koivisto Rune
Tyresö, Sweden
© Courtesy of Claesson Koivisto Rune

Inspired by a typical Swedish barn, this building has a gable roof and rectangular floor plan on two levels, with common spaces on the ground floor and private spaces on the first floor. The open-plan configuration of the 163 m² (1,754 sq ft) interior allows for a very flexible spatial organization.

À l'image de la volumétrie typique de la grange suédoise, ce bâtiment est doté d'une toiture à deux pentes et d'un plan rectangulaire à deux niveaux. Les espaces communs sont situés au rez-de-chaussée et les espaces privés au premier étage. Grâce à la configuration ouverte des intérieurs, qui s'étendent sur 163 m², l'aménagement des espaces est particulièrement flexible.

Dieses Gebäude ist an der typischen schwedischen Volumetrie inspiriert. Es hat ein Satteldach und einen rechteckigen Grundriss auf zwei Ebenen mit gemeinsamen Bereichen im Erdgeschoss und den Privaträumen auf der ersten Etage. Die offene Gestaltung der Innenräume mit insgesamt 163 m² ermöglicht eine sehr flexible Raumaufteilung.

Dit gebouw, dat is gebaseerd op een typisch Zweedse graanschuur, heeft een zadeldak, een rechthoekige plattegrond en twee verdiepingen. De gemeenschappelijke ruimten bevinden zich beneden en de privévertrekken boven. Door de open binnenruimten, in totaal 163 m², is een zeer flexibele, ruimtelijke indeling mogelijk.

Inspirado en la volumetría típica del granero sueco, este edificio presenta una cubierta a dos aguas y planta rectangular de dos niveles, con los espacios comunes en la planta baja y los privados en el primer piso. La configuración abierta de los interiores, de 163 m² en total, permite una organización espacial muy flexible.

Ispirato alla volumetria tipica dei granai svedesi, questo edificio presenta un tetto a due falde e una pianta rettangolare a due livelli, con gli spazi comuni al pianterreno e quelli privati al primo piano. La configurazione aperta degli interni, di 163 m² totali, permette un'organizzazione dello spazio molto flessibile.

Inspirado na volumetria típica de um celeiro sueco, este edifício apresenta um telhado de duas águas e uma estrutura rectangular em dois níveis, com os espaços comuns no piso inferior e os privados no primeiro piso. A configuração aberta dos interiores, de 163 m² no total, permite uma organização espacial muito flexível.

Denna byggnad har inspirerats av den typiska volymetrin hos svenska lador, den har sadeltak och rektangulär planlösning i två våningar, med gemensamma utrymmen på bottenvåningen och de privata utrymmena på övervåningen. Den öppna utformningen av interiören, med totalt 163 m², möjliggör en mycket flexibel användning av ytorna.

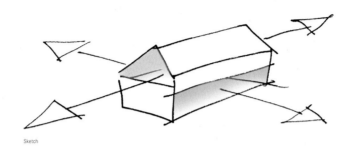

Sketch

Northeast elevation

Southwest elevation

Southeast elevation

Northwest elevation

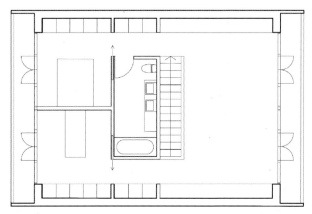

Second floor

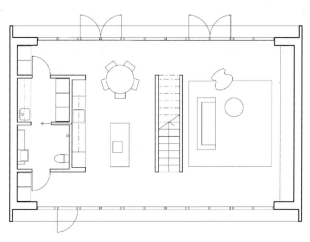

Ground floor

WALL HOUSE

FAR Frohn & Rojas
Santiago de Chile, Chile
© Courtesy of FAR Frohn & Rojas

This 230 m² (2,475 sq ft) low-budget house is an example of energy efficiency during the lifetime of a building. It is organized around a central core and from which up to four different layers are developed. Microclimates are generated among these layers that affect the bioclimatic performance according to season.

Cette maison de 230 m² à petit budget est un exemple d'efficacité énergétique pendant la durée de vie d'un bâtiment. Elle s'organise autour d'un noyau central à partir duquel près de quatre couches différentes s'étendent vers l'extérieur. Entre ces couches, des microclimats se créent et influent sur le fonctionnement bioclimatique selon les saisons.

Dieses 230 m² große Haus mit niedrigem Budget ist ein Beispiel für Energieeffizienz für die Lebensdauer des Gebäudes. Es ist um einen Kern herumgestaltet, von dem aus bis zu vier unterschiedliche Schichten nach außen hin ausgeführt werden. Zwischen dieses Schichten entstehen Mikroklimata, welche die bioklimatische Funktionsweise je nach Jahreszeit beeinflussen.

Deze lowbudgetwoning van 230 m² is een voorbeeld van energetische efficiëntie. Ze is gebouwd rondom een centrale kern waaruit zich naar buiten toe vier verschillende lagen vormen. Tussen die lagen ontwikkelt zich een microklimaat dat afhankelijk van het seizoen de bioklimatologische omstandigheden beïnvloedt.

Esta vivienda de 230 m² y bajo presupuesto es un ejemplo de eficiencia energética durante la vida útil de un edificio. Se organiza en torno a un núcleo central, a partir del cual se desarrollan hacia fuera hasta cuatro capas diferentes. Entre dichas capas se generan microclimas que afectan al funcionamiento bioclimático según la estación del año.

Questa abitazione economica da 230 m² è un esempio di efficienza energetica pianificata per tutta la vita utile di un edificio. Si organizza intorno a un nucleo centrale da cui si sviluppano verso l'esterno fino a quattro strati distinti. Fra questi strati si generano microclimi che modificano il funzionamento bioclimatico a seconda della stagione dell'anno.

Esta casa de 230 m² e orçamento reduzido é um exemplo de eficiência energética durante a vida útil de um edifício. Está organizada em torno de um núcleo central e a partir do qual se desenvolvem quatro camadas diferentes até à parte exterior. Entre as referidas camadas são gerados microclimas que afectam o funcionamento bioclimático de acordo com estação do ano.

Denna lågbudgetbostad på 230 m² är ett exempel på effektiv energiförbrukning under en byggnads livstid. Den har utformats runt en central kärna varifrån upp till fyra olika lager utvecklar sig. Mellan lagren genereras mikroklimat som påverkar det bioklimatiska funktionssättet beroende på årstid.

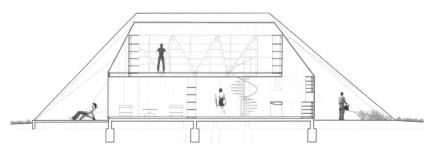

Longitudinal section

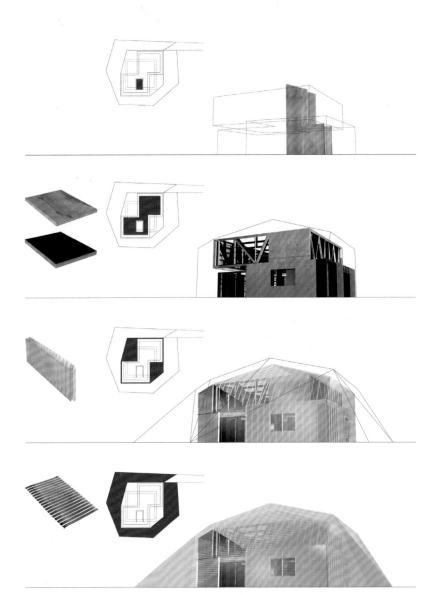

Sketch of construction by layers and materials

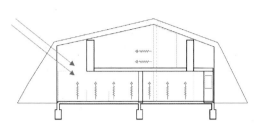

Bioclimatic sketch (winter)

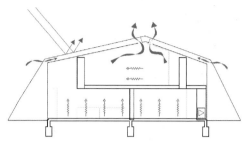

Bioclimatic sketch (summer)

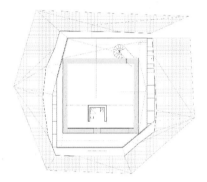

Second floor plan

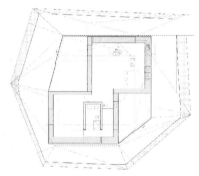

Ground floor plan

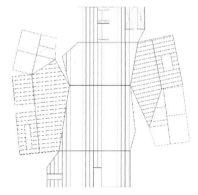

Layer milky shell

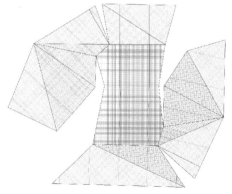

Layer soft skin

269

R. R. HOUSE

Andrade Morettin Associated Architects
Itamambuca, Brazil
© Courtesy of Andrade Morettin Associated Architects

The architects started with the idea of a large shelter in the shape of a shell below which the life of the house will be organized, protected from the intense sun and rain. Similarly, its bioclimatic design should promote cross ventilation. The housing structure is wood, with a prefabricated roof of the same material 6 m (20) ft in height.

Les architectes ont imaginé l'habitation comme un grand refuge en forme de carapace sous lequel s'organiserait la vie de la maison, à l'abri de l'intensité du soleil et des pluies. Toujours dans cet esprit, sa conception bioclimatique visait à favoriser une aération croisée. La structure de la maison est en bois tout comme la toiture préfabriquée située à 6 mètres d'altitude.

Die Architekten gingen von der Grundidee einer großen Hütte im Stil eines Panzers aus, unter dem sich das Leben im Haus geschützt vor der starken Sonne und dem Regen abspielen soll. Auf die gleiche Art sollte der bioklimatische Entwurf die Querbelüftung fördern. Die Struktur des Hauses ist aus Holz mit einem Fertigdach auf 6 Meter Höhe aus dem gleichen Material.

De architecten gingen uit van het idee van een groot toevluchtsoord in de vorm van een schild waaronder zich het huiselijk leven beschermd tegen de elementen afspeelt. Het bioklimatologisch ontwerp moet kruisventilatie bevorderen. Het huis heeft een houten skelet met een prefabdak van hetzelfde materiaal van 6 m hoog.

Los arquitectos partieron de la idea de un gran refugio en forma de caparazón debajo del cual se desarrollara la vida de la casa, protegida del intenso sol y de las lluvias. Del mismo modo, su diseño bioclimático debía potenciar la ventilación cruzada. La estructura de la vivienda es de madera, con una cubierta prefabricada del mismo material a 6 m de altura.

Gli architetti partirono dall'idea di un grande rifugio a forma di guscio, sotto il quale si svolge la vita della casa, al riparo dal sole intenso e dalla pioggia. Allo stesso modo, il suo design bioclimatico doveva potenziare la ventilazione incrociata. La struttura dell'abitazione è in legno, con un rivestimento dello stesso materiale a 6 m di altezza.

Os arquitectos partiram da ideia de um grande refúgio em forma de carapaça sob a qual se desenvolvia a vida da casa, protegida do sol intenso e das chuvas. Do mesmo modo, o seu design bioclimático devia potenciar a ventilação cruzada. A estrutura da casa é de madeira, com uma cobertura pré-fabricada do mesmo material a 6 m de altura.

Arkitekterna utgick från idén om en stor tillflyktsort i form av en sköld under vilken livet i huset försegår, skyddat från den starka solen och regnet. På samma sätt borde dess bioklimatiska utformning främja korsventilationen. Bostadens struktur är av trä, med ett monteringsfärdigt 6 m högt yttertak av samma material.

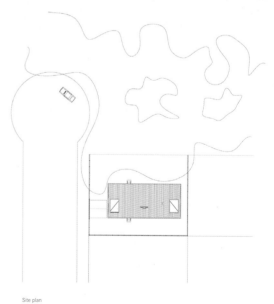

Site plan

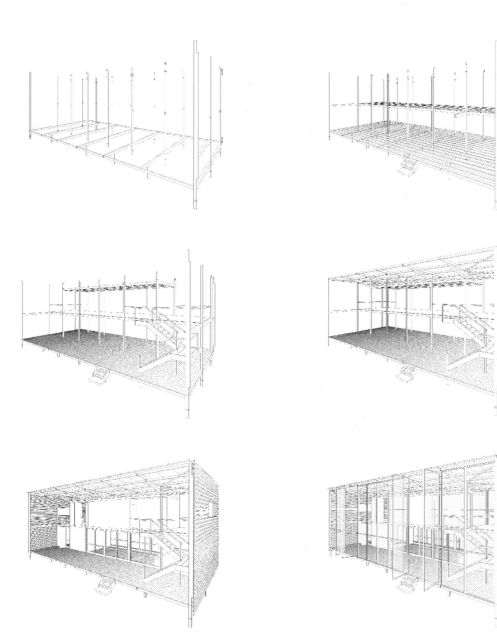

Assembly diagram

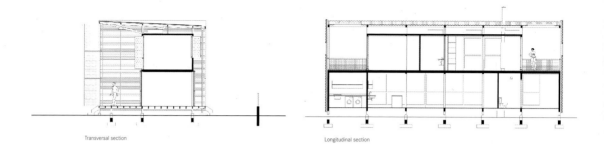

Transversal section

Longitudinal section

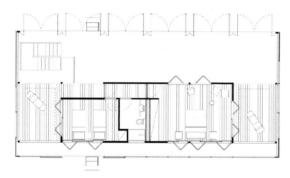

Second floor

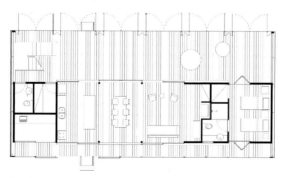

Ground floor

FARLEY STUDIO

M. J. Neal Architects
Cleburne, TX, USA
© Viviane Vives, M. J. Neal

The program is a home-studio covering 228 m² (2,454 sq ft) built on a shoestring budget (111,300 euros). The casing comprises thermally insulated prefabricated steel panels. The coatings also prefabricated, are formed by a double polycarbonate wall and corrugated galvanized steel.

Le programme : une maison-studio de 228 m² construite avec un budget restreint (111 300 euros). La toiture enveloppante est composée d'une structure préfabriquée en acier avec des panneaux isolants thermiques. Les revêtements, également préfabriqués, sont constitués d'un double mur en polycarbonate et en acier galvanisé ondulé.

Das Programm entspricht einer 228 m² großen Studio-Wohnung mit sehr niedrigem Budget (111.300,- Euro). Das umhüllende Dach besteht aus einer Fertigstahlstruktur mit wärmeisolierenden Platten. Die Verkleidungen, die auch Fertigteile sind, bestehen aus einer doppelten Polykarbonatmauer und geriffeltem verzinktem Stahl.

Dit project is een woon-werkruimte van 228 m² die is gebouwd met een zeer beperkt budget (111.300 euro). Het dak bestaat uit een geprefabriceerde stalen constructie met thermisch geïsoleerde panelen. De bekleding, tevens prefab, bestaat uit een dubbele muur van polycarbonaat en gegalvaniseerd gewapend staal.

El programa es una vivienda-estudio de 228 m² construida con un presupuesto muy reducido (111.300 euros). La cubierta envolvente está compuesta por una estructura prefabricada de acero con paneles aislados térmicamente. Los revestimientos, también prefabricados, están formados por un doble muro de policarbonato y acero galvanizado corrugado.

Il programma è un'abitazione-appartamento di 228 m² costruita con un budget ridotto (111.300 euro). La copertura esterna è composta da una struttura prefabbricata in acciaio con pannelli termoisolanti. I rivestimenti, anch'essi prefabbricati, sono formati da un doppio muro di policarbonato e acciaio zincato.

O programa é uma moradia-estúdio de 228 m² construída com um orçamento muito reduzido (111.300 euro). A cobertura envolvente é composta por uma estrutura pré-fabricada de aço com painéis isolados termicamente. Os revestimentos, também pré-fabricados, são constituídos por uma parede dupla de policarbonato e aço galvanizado ondulado.

Programmet är en bostad-studio på 228 m² som är byggd med en mycket låg budget (111 300 euros). Det omslutande yttertaket består av en monteringsfärdig stomme av stål med paneler som är termiskt isolerade. Beklädnaderna, som också är monteringsfärdiga, består av en dubbel vägg av polykarbonat och armeringsstål.

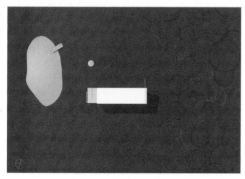

Site plan

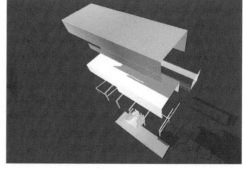

Exploded view

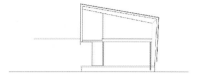

West elevation

North elevation

East elevation

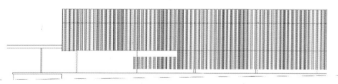

South elevation

HOUSE **S**

Korteknie Stuhlmacher Architecten
Charbonnières-les-Bains, France
© Moritz Bernoully, Olivier Nord, Korteknie Stuhlmacher Architecten

The main space downstairs is a large double height living room topped by a clerestory. The first floor is located at right angles and overhangs. The exterior and interior surfaces are made of wood. The foundations were laid at the site in four weeks, the factory building was completed in four days and the finishing details in six weeks.

L'espace principal du rez-de-chaussée est une grande salle de séjour sur deux niveaux qui donne sur une claire-voie. Le premier étage est situé perpendiculairement et en saillie. Le revêtement extérieur et les surfaces intérieures sont en bois. Quatre semaines ont été nécessaires à l'édification des fondations, quatre jours à la construction en usine et six semaines aux finitions.

Der Hauptraum des Erdgeschosses ist ein großes Wohnzimmer mit doppelter Höhe, das von einem Lichtgaden abgeschlossen ist. Die erste Etage liegt rechtwinklig und fliegend. Außenverkleidung und Innenflächen sind aus Holz. Das Fundament vor Ort wurde in nur vier Wochen gelegt, der Bau im Werk dauerte vier Tage und die Fertigstellung sechs Wochen.

De hoofdruimte van de benedenverdieping is een grote woonkamer van dubbele hoogte die uitloopt in een lichtbeuk. De eerste verdieping ligt loodrecht op de begane grond en steekt uit. De binnen- en buitenkant zijn bekleed met hout. Het leggen van de fundering duurde vier weken, de vervaardiging in de fabriek vier dagen en de afwerking zes weken.

El espacio principal de la planta baja es una gran sala de estar de doble altura rematada por un claristorio. La primera planta está situada en perpendicular y en voladizo. El revestimiento exterior y las superficies interiores son de madera. La cimentación en el emplazamiento duró cuatro semanas, la construcción en fábrica se realizó en cuatro días y los acabados, en seis semanas.

Lo spazio principale al pianterreno è un gran salone a doppia altezza sormontato da un cleristorio. Il primo piano è disposto in perpendicolare ed è aggettante. Il rivestimento esterno e le superfici interne sono in legno. Le fondazioni in situ durarono quattro settimane, la costruzione in fabbrica venne realizzata in quattro giorni e le finiture in sei settimane.

O espaço principal do piso inferior é uma grande sala de estar com altura dupla rematada por um clerestório. O primeiro piso está situado na perpendicular e em vão. O revestimento exterior e as superfícies interiores são de madeira. As fundações no local duraram quatro semanas, a produção em fábrica foi realizada em quatro dias e os acabamentos em seis semanas.

Det största utrymmet på bottenplan är ett stort vardagsrum med dubbel höjd som avslutas med ett klerestorium. Övervåningen ligger i vinkelrät linje och i utsprång. Den utvändiga beklädnaden och de invändiga ytorna är av trä. Grunden och placeringen tog fyra veckor, tillverkningen på fabrik gjordes på fyra dagar och finishen tog sex veckor.

Site plan

Second floor

Ground floor

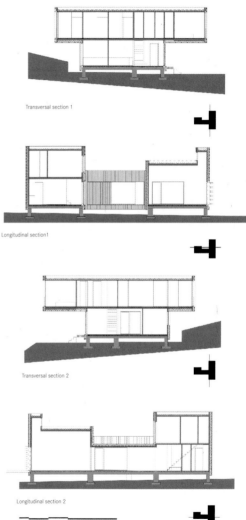

Transversal section 1

Longitudinal section1

Transversal section 2

Longitudinal section 2

GLIDEHOUSE

MKD-Michelle Kaufmann Designs
Novato, CA, USA
© John Swain

The Glidehouse model belongs to a series of modular homes designed in a sustainable manner. In addition to their prefabricated nature, this model presents several environmental measures: a solar PV system, the use of certified wood (FSC) in the structure and finishes, bamboo flooring and recycled glass tiles in the bathroom.

Le modèle Glidehouse fait partie d'une série de maisons modulaires conçues de manière durable. Outre son caractère préfabriqué, diverses mesures environnementales sont intégrées dans ce modèle : un système d'énergie solaire photovoltaïque, l'utilisation de bois certifié (FSC) pour la structure et les finitions, des sols en bambou et des carreaux en verre recyclé dans la salle de bains.

Das Glidehouse-Modell gehört zu einer Reihe modularer Häuser, die mit nachhaltigem Stil entwickelt wurden. Neben seiner Fertigbauweise zeigt dieses Modell unterschiedliche umweltfreundliche Maßnahmen: Fotovoltaiksolarenergie, Verwendung von zertifiziertem Holz (FSC) an der Struktur und an den Ausführungen, Böden aus Bambus und Platten aus recyceltem Glas im Bad.

Model Glidehouse behoort tot een reeks modulaire huizen met duurzaam ontwerp. Naast het feit dat het hier om een prefabwoning gaat, beschikt het over verschillende milieuvriendelijke voorzieningen: een systeem voor zonne-energie, het gebruik van gecertificeerd hout (FSC) voor het skelet en de afwerking, vloeren van bamboe en plavuizen van recycled glas in de badkamer.

El modelo Glidehouse pertenece a una serie de casas modulares diseñadas de manera sostenible. Además de su carácter prefabricado, este modelo presenta diversas medidas medioambientales: sistema de energía solar fotovoltaica, uso de madera certificada (FSC) en la estructura y los acabados, suelos de bambú y baldosas de vidrio reciclado en el baño.

Il modello Glidehouse appartiene a una serie di case modulari progettate in modo sostenibile. Oltre ad essere prefabbricato, questo modello presenta diverse misure a favore dell'ambiente: un impianto fotovoltaico, l'uso di legno certificato (FSC) sia per la struttura che per le finiture, pavimenti in bambù e piastrelle in vetro riciclato per il bagno.

O modelo Glidehouse pertence a uma série de casas modulares desenhadas de forma sustentável. Além do seu carácter pré-fabricado, este modelo apresenta diversas medidas ambientais: um sistema de energia solar fotovoltaica, a utilização de madeira certificada (FSC) na estrutura e nos acabamentos, chão de bambu e azulejos de vidro reciclado na casa de banho.

Modellen Glidehouse tillhör en serie modulhus som är formgivna på ett hållbart sätt. Förutom dess monteringsfärdiga egenskap, har denna modell flera miljömässiga åtgärder. Ett system med fotovoltaisk solenergi, användning av certifierat trä (FSC) i stommen och finishen, golv av bambu och klinkerplattor av återvunnet glas i badrummet.

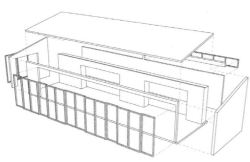

Factory production

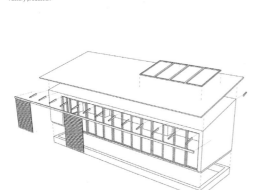

On site button up

Completed Glidehouse

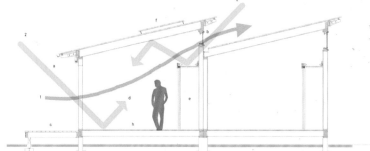

a. Sliding glass door wall
b. Clerestory windows
c. Outdoor room
d. Indoor living
e. Storage bar with shelving behind sliding wood doors
f. Solar panels
g. Bamboo flooring
1. Cross-ventilation in all the main spaces
2. Balanced daylighting/indirect lighting

Bioclimatic section

Floor plan

RUCKSACK HOUSE

Stefan Eberstadt
Leipzig and Cologne, Germany
© Claus Bach, Stefan Eberstadt, Hana Schäfer, Thomas Taubert, Silke Koch

The prototype is a cube shape and is suspended by steel cables anchored to the roof and the façade of the building which is parasitic. The interior is entirely clad in birch plywood. It features folding furniture that once unfolded, can provide shelves, desk or a bed.

Ce prototype présente une forme de cube, qui est suspendu à l'aide de câbles en acier ancrés à la toiture et à la façade du bâtiment, auquel il vient s'ajouter. L'intérieur, entièrement revêtu d'un contreplaqué en bouleau, présente un mobilier modulable qui, une fois déplié, peut servir d'étagère, de bureau ou de lit pour dormir.

Der Prototyp ist in Würfelform errichtet und mit am Dach und an der Gebäudefassade verankerten Stahlseilen wie ein Parasit davon aufgehängt. Der Innenraum ist vollständig mit Birkenfurnier verkleidet. Die Möbel sind zusammenklappbar und können im aufgeklappten Zustand als Regal, Schreibtisch oder Bett dienen.

Het prototype is een kubusvorm die aan stalen kabels hangt die zijn verankerd aan het dak en de gevel van het gebouw waar het als een parasiet aan vastzit. Het interieur is volledig afgewerkt met berken plaatmateriaal. Het opvouwbare meubilair kan zich ontplooien tot boekenkast, bureau of bed.

El prototipo presenta forma de cubo y está suspendido por cables de acero ancorados a la cubierta y a la fachada del edificio del cual es parásito. El interior está enteramente revestido con contrachapado de abedul. Presenta mobiliario plegable que, una vez desplegado, puede ofrecer estanterías, escritorio o lecho para dormir.

Il prototipo è a forma di cubo ed è sospeso mediante cavi in acciaio ancorati al tetto e alla facciata dell'edificio di cui è parassita. L'interno è interamente rivestito in compensato di betulla. È dotato di mobili pieghevoli che, una volta aperti, offrono degli scaffali, una scrivania e un letto per dormire.

O protótipo apresenta forma de cubo e está suspensa por cabos de aço ancorados ao telhado e à fachada do edifício do qual é parasita. O interior é inteiramente revestido em contraplacado de bétula. Possui mobiliário desdobrável que quando aberto, pode fornecer prateleiras, secretária ou cama.

Prototypen visar en kubisk form och den hänger i stålkablar som är förankrade i skyddstaket och i byggnadens fasad på vilken den är parasit. Interiören är helt klädd med björkfaner. Den har ett hopfällbart möblemang som, när det är uppfällt, kan fungera som bokhyllor, skrivbord eller säng.

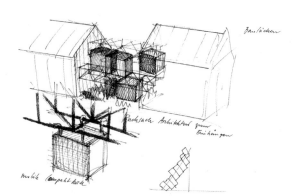

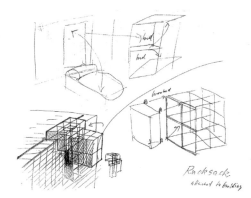

Sketches

Rear anchoring with steel cable section

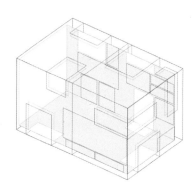

Axonometric view

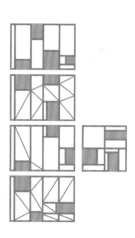

Measurements of the different parts
which make up the prototype

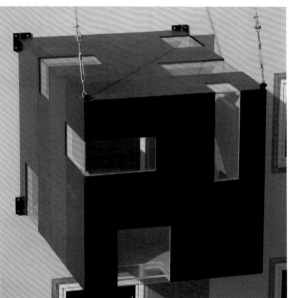

LAKE SEYMOUR GETAWAY

UCArchitect
Marmora, Canada
© UCArchitect

A wooden L-shaped screen defines the access points and draws a circular path through the façade. Between the interior and exterior a link has been created that is accentuated by the use of skylights, eaves and large openings substituting the windows. The interior space is configured around a hub integrating the kitchen and bathroom.

Un panneau en bois en forme de L indique l'accès et dessine un chemin circulaire à travers la façade. Le lien qui a été créé entre intérieur et extérieur est mis en avant par l'utilisation de lucarnes, d'avant-toits et de grandes ouvertures qui remplacent les fenêtres. L'espace intérieur s'articule autour d'un noyau qui comprend la cuisine et la salle de bains.

Ein Holzschirm in L-Form kennzeichnet den Zugang und zeichnet einen kreisförmigen Weg durch die Fassade hindurch. Zwischen Innen- und Außenbereich wurde eine Verbindung geschaffen, die durch den Einsatz von Dachluken, Flügeln und großen Öffnungen, welche die Fenster ersetzen, betont wurde. Der Innenraum wurde um einen Kern herumgestaltet, der Küche und Bad enthält.

Een houten paneel in de vorm van een L geeft de toegang tot de woning aan en trekt een cirkelvormig pad over de gevel. De binnen- en buitenruimte zijn met elkaar verbonden, wat versterkt wordt door het gebruik van dakvensters, overhangende dankranden en grote openingen in plaats van ramen. De binnenruimte bevindt zich rondom een kern waarin zich de keuken en badkamer bevinden.

Una pantalla de madera en forma de L señala el acceso y traza un camino circular a través de la fachada. Entre el interior y el exterior se ha creado un vínculo que se acentúa mediante el uso de claraboyas, aleros y grandes aberturas que sustituyen a las ventanas. El espacio interior se ha configurado alrededor de un núcleo que integra la cocina y el baño.

Uno schermo in legno a forma di L segnala l'accesso e traccia un percorso circolare attraverso la facciata. Tra l'interno e l'esterno è stato creato un vincolo che si accentua con l'uso di lucernari, grondaie e grandi aperture che sostituiscono le finestre. Lo spazio interno è stato configurato attorno ad un nucleo che integra la cucina e il bagno.

Uma tela de madeira em forma de L identifica o acesso e traça um caminho circular através da fachada. Foi criada uma ligação entre o interior e no exterior, reforçada através da utilização de claraboias, beirais e grandes aberturas que substituem as janelas. O espaço interior foi configurado à volta de um núcleo que integra a cozinha e a casa de banho.

En L-formad träskärm visar ingången och skissar en rund väg genom fasaden. Mellan det invändiga och det utvändiga har en förbindelse skapats, som betonas genom användning av takfönster, takutsprång och stora öppningar som ersätter fönster. De invändiga ytorna har formats runt kärnan som utgörs av köket och badrummet.

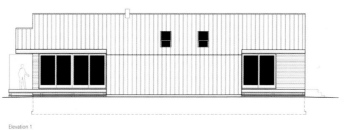

Elevation 1

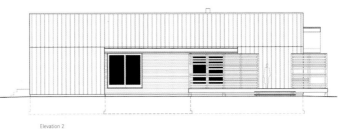

Elevation 2

Section A

Section B

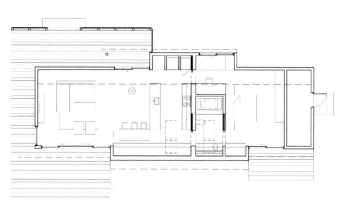

Floor plan

CABIN **VARDEHAUGEN**

Fantastic Norway Architects
Åfjord, Norway
© Fantastic Norway Architects

This cabin, located at 35 m (114 ft) above sea level, is located on the Fosen peninsula. In this harsh climate landscape rocks, sea and mountain are predominant features. The structure of the small house is based on the organization of traditional Norwegian towns, small urban hubs that are characterized by the semi-air conditioning of outdoor spaces.

Cette cabane, située à 35 mètres au-dessus du niveau de la mer, se situe dans la péninsule de Fosen. Les roches, la mer et la montagne dominent ce paysage marqué par un climat rude. La structure de la petite maison se fonde sur l'organisation des villages norvégiens traditionnels : de petits noyaux urbains caractérisés par la semi-climatisation des espaces extérieurs.

Diese 35 m über dem Meeresspiegel gelegene Hütte befindet sich auf der Fosen-Halbinsel. In dieser Landschaft mit rauem Klima herrschen Felsen, Meer und Gebirge vor. Der Aufbau des kleinen Hauses basiert auf der Organisation traditioneller norwegischer Dörfer, d. h. kleinen Ortskernen, die sich durch die Halbklimatisierung der Außenbereiche kennzeichnen.

Deze blokhut op 35 meter boven zeeniveau staat op het schiereiland Fosen (Noorwegen). In dit ruwe klimaat wordt het landschap overheerst door rotsen, zee en bergen. De constructie van deze kleine woning is gebaseerd op de indeling van traditionele Noorse dorpjes, kleine woonkernen waarin de buitenruimten gedeeltelijke klimatologische beheersing kennen.

Esta cabaña, situada a 35 m sobre el nivel del mar, se encuentra en la península de Fosen. En este paisaje de clima áspero dominan las rocas, el mar y el monte. La estructura de la pequeña vivienda se basa en la organización de los pueblos noruegos tradicionales, pequeños núcleos urbanos que se caracterizan por la semiclimatización de los espacios exteriores.

Questa abitazione, situata a 35 m sul livello del mare, si trova sulla penisola di Fosen. Questo paesaggio dal clima aspro è dominato da rocce, mare e montagne. La struttura di questa casetta si basa sull'organizzazione dei paesi tradizionali norvegesi, piccoli nuclei urbani caratterizzati dalla semiclimatizzazione degli spazi esterni.

Esta cabana, situada a 35 m acima do nível do mar, situa-se na península de Fosen. Nesta paisagem de clima áspero dominam as rochas, o mar e a montanha. A estrutura da pequena casa baseia-se na organização dos povos noruegueses tradicionais, pequenos núcleos urbanos que se caracterizam pela semi-climatização dos espaços exteriores.

Denna stuga som ligger 35 m över havsytan, ligger på Fosenhalvön. I detta landskap med strävt klimat dominerar klipporna, havet och bergen. Den lilla bostadens stomme grundas på organisation av de traditionella norska byarna, små stadskärnor som karaktäriseras av semiluftkonditionering av de utvändiga ytorna.

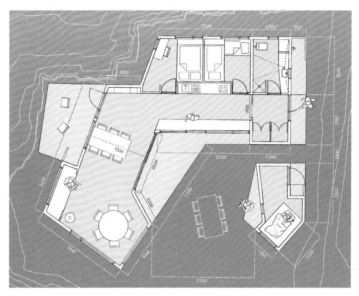

Floor plan

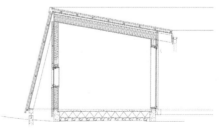

Sections

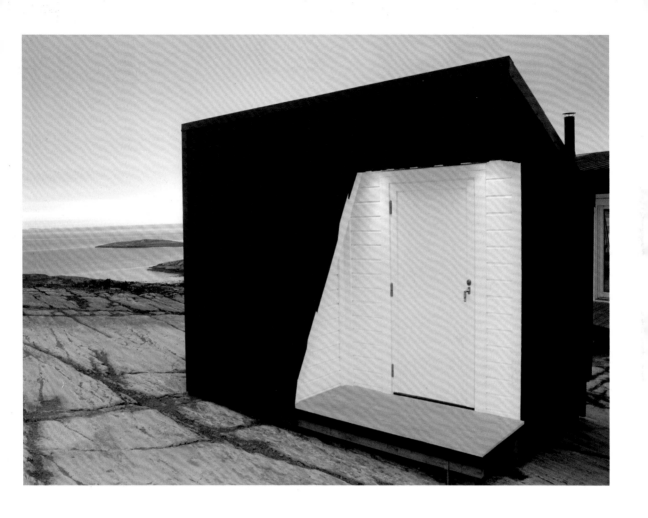

CASA **LARGA**

Daniele Claudio Taddei
Brissago, Switzerland
© Bruno Helbling

This house is situated in the middle of a vineyard perfectly integrated with the environment. Its elegant structure is reminiscent of farm buildings in the area. Access to the building is through the basement floor and reaches four stories. The vertical lines dominate the façade where the rhythmic location of the windows stands out.

Cette maison a été construite au milieu de vignes en s'intégrant parfaitement à son environnement. Son élégante structure rappelle les bâtiments agricoles de la région. Le bâtiment, de quatre étages, est accessible par le sous-sol et présente une façade, où dominent les lignes verticales et une distribution régulière des fenêtres.

Das Haus steht, einwandfrei in sein Umfeld integriert, mitten in einem Weinberg. Seine elegante Struktur erinnert an die Landwirtschaftsgebäude des Gebiets. Der Zugang zum vier Etagen hohen Gebäude erfolgt in der unterirdischen Etage. Auf der Fassade, auf der die rhythmische Anordnung der Fenster betont ist, herrschen senkrechte Linien vor.

Dit huis ligt midden in een perfect in de omgeving geïntegreerde wijngaard. De elegante constructie doet denken aan de agrarische gebouwen in het gebied. De toegang tot het huis bevindt zich bij de ondergrondse verdieping en biedt toegang tot vier woonlagen. In de voorgevel, die wordt gedomineerd door verticale lijnen, valt de ritmische plaatsing van de ramen op.

Esta casa se sitúa en medio de una viña perfectamente integrada con el entorno. Su estructura elegante recuerda a los edificios agrícolas de la zona. El acceso al edificio se encuentra en el piso subterráneo y alcanza cuatro pisos. Las líneas verticales dominan en la fachada donde destaca la ubicación rítmica de las ventanas.

Questa casa si trova al centro di un vigneto, perfettamente integrata con l'ambiente circostante. La sua elegante struttura ricorda i fabbricati agricoli della zona. L'accesso si trova al piano sotterraneo e conta in tutto quattro piani. Le linee verticali dominano la facciata, in cui spicca la posizione ritmica delle finestre.

Esta casa situa-se no meio de uma vinha perfeitamente integrada com o ambiente. A sua estrutura elegante relembra os edifícios agrícolas da zona. O acesso ao edifício encontra-se no piso subterrâneo e atinge quatro andares. As linhas verticais dominam a fachada onde a localização rítmica das janelas sobressai.

Detta hus är beläget mitt i en vingård som är perfekt integrerad i omgivningen. Dess eleganta struktur påminner om jordbruksbyggnaderna i området. Byggnadens ingång ligger på suterrängvåningen och den har fyra våningar. De lodräta linjerna dominerar på fasaden där den rytmiska placeringen av fönster utmärker sig.

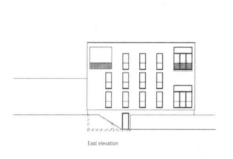

East elevation

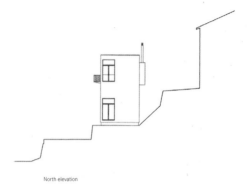

North elevation

South elevation

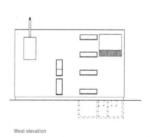

West elevation

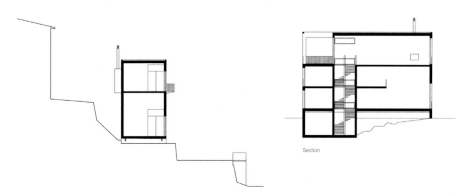

Atelier section

Section

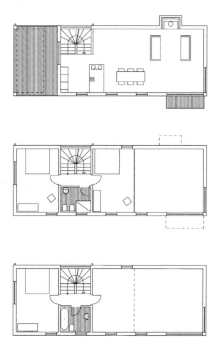

Floor plans

BRIDGE HOUSE

Max Pritchard Architect
Ash Bourne, Australia
© Sam Noonan

Customers needed a permanent home and studio. The structure supports a concrete slab and on it stands the house, just over 100 m² (1,076 sq ft). The structure and shape of the house reduces the ecological footprint on the land. The black concrete of the floor stores heat thanks to its thermal mass and double glazing retain it.

Les clients avaient besoin d'une maison et d'un bureau permanent. Cette structure supporte une dalle en béton, sur laquelle se dresse l'habitation, d'une surface légèrement supérieure à 100 m². La structure et la forme de la maison réduisent l'impact environnemental sur le terrain. Le béton noir du plancher emmagasine de la chaleur grâce à sa masse thermique et le double vitrage permet de la conserver.

Die Kunden brauchten eine permanente Wohnung und ein Studio. Die Struktur trägt eine Betonplatte, auf der die Wohnung mit etwas über 100 m² Größe aufliegt. Struktur und Form des Hauses reduzieren die ökologischen Auswirkungen auf das Gelände. Der schwarze Beton am Boden sammelt dank seiner Wärmemasse Wärme und die doppelt verglasten Fenster halten sie zurück.

De klant wenste een permanente woning met studio. De constructie bestaat uit een grote betonnen plaat waarop de woning rust, die een oppervlakte heeft van iets meer dan 100 m². Door de gekozen constructie en de vorm van het huis is de ecologische belasting van het terrein relatief laag. Het zwarte beton van de vloer bouwt warmte op dankzij zijn thermische massa en de dubbele beglazing houdt de warmte vast.

Los clientes necesitaban una vivienda y estudio permanente. La estructura soporta una losa de hormigón y sobre ella se alza la vivienda, de poco más de 100 m². La estructura y la forma de la casa reduce la huella ecológica en el terreno. El hormigón negro del suelo acumula calor gracias a su masa térmica y los dobles cristales lo retienen.

I clienti volevano un'abitazione e uno studio permanente. La struttura sostiene una lastra di cemento, su cui si trova la casa, di poco più di 100 m². La struttura e la forma della casa riducono l'impronta ecologica sul terreno. Il pavimento in cemento nero assorbe il calore grazie alla sua massa termica e i doppi vetri lo conservano.

Os clientes necessitavam de uma casa e estúdio permanente. A estrutura suporta uma laje de betão e sobre ela se ergue a casa, de pouco mais de 100 m². A estrutura e a forma da casa reduz a pegada ecológica no terreno. O betão preto do chão acumula calor graças à sua massa térmica e aos vidros duplos retém-no.

Kunderna behövde en permanent bostad och studio. Stommen bär upp en stenplatta av betong och över den reser sig bostaden som är lite mer än 100 m². Stommen och husets form minskar miljöpåverkan på området. Den svarta betongen ackumulerar värme tack vara sin termiska massa och dubbla glas håller kvar värmen.

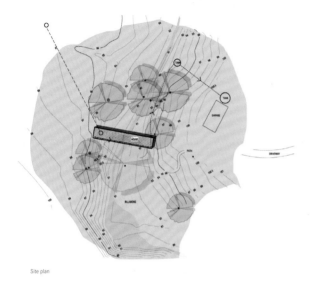

Site plan

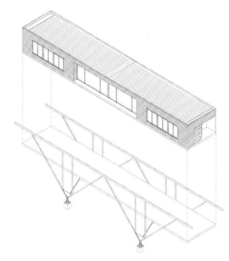

Axonometric view of the structure

Floor plan

RESIDENTIAL CONTAINERS

Petr Hájek Architekti
Prague, Czech Republic
© Ester Havlova

This extension was performed with two containers on the roof of a building in Prague as if they were wedges. The new spaces contain the living areas. An electronic system controls the sunlight that enters the house and regulates temperature automatically opening or closing the blinds.

L'agrandissement de cette habitation a été réalisé avec deux containers encastrés dans le toit d'un bâtiment de Prague, comme si c'étaient des cales. Les nouveaux espaces abritent les zones habitables. Un système électronique contrôle la lumière du soleil qui pénètre dans la maison et régule la température en ouvrant ou fermant automatiquement les stores.

Diese Erweiterung erfolgte mit zwei Containern, die auf dem Dach eines Gebäudes in Prag eingesetzt wurden, als ob es sich um Keile handelte. Die neuen Räumlichkeiten enthalten die bewohnbaren Bereiche. Ein elektronisches System überwacht das in das Haus eindringende Sonnenlicht und regelt die Temperatur, indem es die Rollläden automatisch öffnet und schließt.

Deze uitbreiding is gerealiseerd met twee containers die op het dak van een gebouw in Praag zijn geplaatst, alsof het blokken zijn. De nieuwe ruimten verbinden de bewoonbare delen met elkaar. Een elektronisch systeem regelt de hoeveelheid zonlicht die in huis valt en reguleert de temperatuur door de rolluiken automatisch open of dicht te doen.

Esta ampliación se ha realizado con dos contenedores encajados en el tejado de un edificio de Praga como si se tratara de unas cuñas. Los nuevos espacios reúnen las áreas habitables. Un sistema electrónico controla la luz del sol que entra en la casa y regula la temperatura abriendo o cerrando automáticamente las persianas.

Questa estensione è stata realizzata con due container incassati sul tetto di un edificio di Praga, come se fossero cunei. I nuovi spazi riuniscono le zone abitabili. Un sistema elettronico controlla la luce del sole che entra nella casa e regola la temperatura automaticamente aprendo o chiudendo le persiane.

Esta ampliação realizou-se com dois contentores encaixados no telhado de um edifício de Praga como se fosse umas cunhas. Os novos espaços reúnem as áreas habitáveis. Um sistema electrónico controla a luz do sol que entra na casa e regula a temperatura abrindo ou fechando automaticamente as persianas.

Denna tillbyggnad har gjorts med två containrar som är sammanfogade i taket, i en byggnad i Prag, som om det vore ett par kilar. De nya utrymmena sammanför de beboliga områdena. Ett elektriskt system kontrollerar solljuset som kommer in i huset och reglerar temperaturen genom att automatiskt öppna och stänga jalusierna.

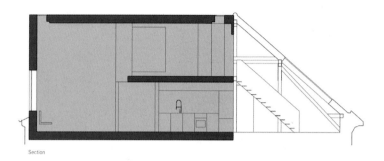

Section

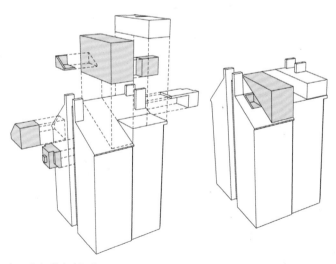

Axonometric view of the inserted containers

RESTORED **FARMHOUSE**

Jeffrey McKean Architect
Claryville, NY, USA
© Keith Mendenhall/Jeffrey McKean Architect

This farm, built with Canadian hemlock was in very bad condition, and urgent action was needed. The annex is a simple rectilinear volume paneled with recycled and FSC certified cedar wood. Varnishes and paints used in the rehabilitation of wood and soils have low levels of volatile organic compounds (VOCs).

Cette ferme, construite en bois de tsuga ou cigüe, était en très mauvais état et nécessitait donc une intervention urgente. L'annexe est un volume rectiligne et simple, revêtu de bois recyclé et de cèdre certifié FSC. Les vernis et peintures utilisés pour la rénovation des bois et des sols contiennent des niveaux faibles de composés organiques volatils (COV).

Dieser Bauernhof, der aus Tsuga canadensis- oder Cicutaholz erbaut ist, befand sich in einem sehr schlechten Zustand und ein dringender Eingriff war erforderlich. Der Anbau ist ein geradliniges und einfaches, mit recyceltem und zertifiziertem FSC–Zedernholz verkleidetes Volumen. Die bei der Wiederherstellung der Hölzer und Böden verwendeten Lacke und Farben besitzen geringe Mengen flüchtiger organischer Bestandteile.

Deze boerderij, gebouwd van tsuga- of cicutahout, was in slechte staat, waardoor er dringend iets gedaan moest worden. Het bijgebouw is een eenvoudig, rechtlijnig deel bekleed met gerecycled cederhout met FSC-keurmerk. De lak en verf die zijn gebruikt bij de restauratie van het houtwerk en de vloeren bevat lage doses vluchtige organische stoffen (VOS).

Esta granja, construida con madera de tsuga o cicuta, se encontraba en muy mal estado, por lo que era necesaria una actuación urgente. El anexo es un volumen rectilíneo y sencillo revestido de madera reciclada y de cedro certificado FSC. Los barnices y pinturas utilizados en la rehabilitación de las maderas y los suelos poseen bajos niveles de compuestos orgánicos volátiles (COV).

Questa fattoria, costruita con legno di hemlock era in pessime condizioni, tanto da rendere necessario un intervento urgente. L'aggiunta è un semplice volume rettilineo rivestito in legno riciclato e cedro certificato FSC. Le vernici utilizzate per il restauro del legno e dei pavimenti hanno bassi livelli di composti organici volatili (COV).

Esta granja, construída com madeira de tsuga ou cicuta, encontrava-se em muito mau estado, pelo que era necessária uma actuação urgente. O anexo é um volume rectilíneo e simples revestido de madeira reciclada e de cedro certificado FSC. Os vernizes e pinturas utilizados na reabilitação das madeiras e dos pavimentos possuem baixos níveis de compostos orgânicos voláteis (COV).

Denna gård som är byggd av trä från hemlock eller sprängört var i mycket dåligt skick, och därför var det nödvändigt med brådskande åtgärder. Anexet är en rätlinjig och enkel volym som är klädd med återvunnet trä och FSC-certifierat cederträ. Lacker och målarfärger som har använts i återuppbyggnaden av trä och golv har låga nivåer av flyktiga organiska föreningar (VOC).

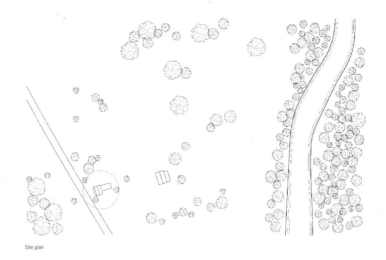

Site plan

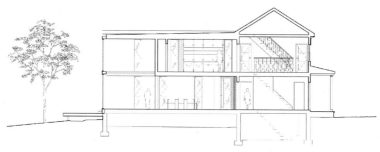

Longitudinal section

Elevation

Elevations

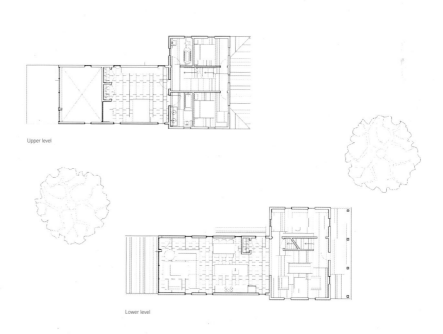

Upper level

Lower level

PECONIC BAY HOUSE

Resolution: 4 Architecture
Shinnecock Hills, NY, USA
© Resolution: 4 Architecture

The main volume of the house is protected with cedarwood of warm tones and the outdoors area has a cement lining. Photovoltaic solar panels installed on the roof and the use of geothermal energy make the house its own power plant that also supplies power to the network daily.

Le volume principal du logement est protégé par du bois de cèdre dans des tons chauds et la zone extérieure présente un revêtement en ciment. Les panneaux solaires photovoltaïques installés sur le toit et l'utilisation d'énergie géothermique font de cette maison sa propre centrale d'énergie qui, de plus, fournit quotidiennement de l'énergie au réseau.

Der größte Teil des Hauses ist mit Zedernholz in warmen Farbtönen geschützt und der Außenbereich ist mit Zement verkleidet. Die auf dem Dach installierten Fotovoltaikplatten und die Nutzung der Energie aus Erdwärme verwandeln das Haus in sein eigenes Erzeugerwerk, das außerdem täglich Strom in das Netz einspeißt.

Het hoofddeel van de woning wordt beschermd met cederhout in warme tinten en het uitstekende deel is bekleed met cement. De zonnepanelen op het dak en het gebruik van geothermische energie veranderen de woning in een soort eigen energiecentrale die ook nog eens dagelijks energie aan het net afgeeft.

El volumen principal de la vivienda está protegido con madera de cedro de tonos cálidos y la zona exterior tiene un revestimiento de cemento. Los paneles solares fotovoltaicos instalados en la cubierta y el uso de energía geotérmica convierten la casa en su propia planta generadora, que, además, suministra energía a la red diariamente.

Il volume principale dell'abitazione è protetto con legno di cedro dai toni caldi e l'esterno ha un rivestimento di cemento. Grazie ai pannelli solari fotovoltaici installati sul tetto e all'uso di energia geotermica questa casa è come un generatore autosufficiente che in più alimenta la rete elettrica ogni giorno.

O volume principal da casa é protegido com madeira de cedro de tons quentes e a zona exterior apresenta um revestimento de betão. Os painéis solares fotovoltaicos instalados na cobertura e a utilização de energia geotérmica convertem a casa na sua própria planta geradora que, fornece ainda, energia à rede diariamente.

Den viktigaste volymen i denna bostad skyddas med cederträ i varma toner och utomhusområdet har en cementbeklädnad. De fotovoltaiska solfångarna som har installerats på taket och användningen av geotermisk energi förvandlar huset till sin egen energianläggning som dessutom levererar energi till nätet dagligen.

West elevation

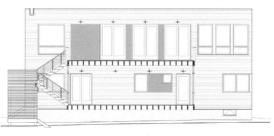

South elevation

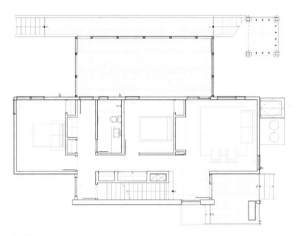

Lower level

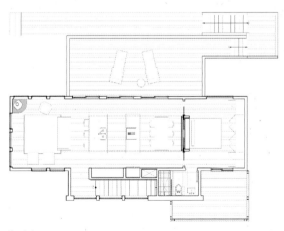

Upper level